OPPOSING
VIEWPOINTS®
SERIES

The Armed Forces

Other Books of Related Interest:

Opposing Viewpoints Series

Veterans

At Issue Series

Homeland Security

Current Controversies Series

Disaster Response

"Congress shall make no law . . . abridging the freedom of speech, or of the press."

First Amendment to the U.S. Constitution

The basic foundation of our democracy is the First Amendment guarantee of freedom of expression. The Opposing Viewpoints Series is dedicated to the concept of this basic freedom and the idea that it is more important to practice it than to enshrine it.

OPPOSING
VIEWPOINTS®
SERIES

The Armed Forces

Louise I. Gerdes, book editor

GREENHAVEN PRESS
A part of Gale, Cengage Learning

GALE
CENGAGE Learning™

Detroit • New York • San Francisco • New Haven, Conn • Waterville, Maine • London

Christine Nasso, *Publisher*
Elizabeth Des Chenes, *Managing Editor*

© 2010 Greenhaven Press, a part of Gale, Cengage Learning.

For more information, contact:
Greenhaven Press
27500 Drake Rd.
Farmington Hills, MI 48331-3535
Or you can visit our Internet site at gale.cengage.com

Articles in Greenhaven Press anthologies are often edited for length to meet page requirements. In addition, original titles of these works are changed to clearly present the main thesis and to explicitly indicate the author's opinion. Every effort is made to ensure that Greenhaven Press accurately reflects the original intent of the authors. Every effort has been made to trace the owners of copyrighted material.

Cover Image copyright Purestock/Getty Images.

LIBRARY OF CONGRESS CATALOGING-IN-PUBLICATION DATA

The armed forces / Louise I. Gerdes, book editor.
   p. cm. -- (Opposing viewpoints)
   Includes bibliographical references and index.
   ISBN 978-0-7377-4755-3 (hardcover) -- ISBN 978-0-7377-4756-0 (pbk.)
   1. Armed Forces--Juvenile literature. 2. Military policy--Juvenile literature. I. Gerdes, Louise I., 1953-
   UA10.A74 2010
   355'.0335--dc22

                2009053675

Printed in the United States of America
1 2 3 4 5 6 7 14 13 12 11 10

Contents

Chapter 2: Who Should Serve in the Armed Forces?

Chapter 3: How Should Armed Forces Resources Be Managed?

Chapter 4: What Policies Best Govern Armed Forces Personnel?

Why Consider Opposing Viewpoints?

> *"The only way in which a human being can make some approach to knowing the whole of a subject is by hearing what can be said about it by persons of every variety of opinion and studying all modes in which it can be looked at by every character of mind. No wise man ever acquired his wisdom in any mode but this."*
>
> *John Stuart Mill*

In our media-intensive culture it is not difficult to find differing opinions. Thousands of newspapers and magazines and dozens of radio and television talk shows resound with differing points of view. The difficulty lies in deciding which opinion to agree with and which "experts" seem the most credible. The more inundated we become with differing opinions and claims, the more essential it is to hone critical reading and thinking skills to evaluate these ideas. Opposing Viewpoints books address this problem directly by presenting stimulating debates that can be used to enhance and teach these skills. The varied opinions contained in each book examine many different aspects of a single issue. While examining these conveniently edited opposing views, readers can develop critical thinking skills such as the ability to compare and contrast authors' credibility, facts, argumentation styles, use of persuasive techniques, and other stylistic tools. In short, the Opposing Viewpoints Series is an ideal way to attain the higher-level thinking and reading skills so essential in a culture of diverse and contradictory opinions.

In addition to providing a tool for critical thinking, Opposing Viewpoints books challenge readers to question their own strongly held opinions and assumptions. Most people form their opinions on the basis of upbringing, peer pressure, and personal, cultural, or professional bias. By reading carefully balanced opposing views, readers must directly confront new ideas as well as the opinions of those with whom they disagree. This is not to argue simplistically that everyone who reads opposing views will—or should—change his or her opinion. Instead, the series enhances readers' understanding of their own views by encouraging confrontation with opposing ideas. Careful examination of others' views can lead to the readers' understanding of the logical inconsistencies in their own opinions, perspective on why they hold an opinion, and the consideration of the possibility that their opinion requires further evaluation.

Evaluating Other Opinions

To ensure that this type of examination occurs, Opposing Viewpoints books present all types of opinions. Prominent spokespeople on different sides of each issue as well as well-known professionals from many disciplines challenge the reader. An additional goal of the series is to provide a forum for other, less known, or even unpopular viewpoints. The opinion of an ordinary person who has had to make the decision to cut off life support from a terminally ill relative, for example, may be just as valuable and provide just as much insight as a medical ethicist's professional opinion. The editors have two additional purposes in including these less known views. One, the editors encourage readers to respect others' opinions—even when not enhanced by professional credibility. It is only by reading or listening to and objectively evaluating others' ideas that one can determine whether they are worthy of consideration. Two, the inclusion of such viewpoints encourages the important critical thinking skill of objectively evaluating an author's credentials and bias. This evaluation will illuminate an author's reasons for taking a particular stance on an issue and will aid in readers' evaluation of the author's ideas.

It is our hope that these books will give readers a deeper understanding of the issues debated and an appreciation of the complexity of even seemingly simple issues when good and honest people disagree. This awareness is particularly important in a democratic society such as ours in which people enter into public debate to determine the common good. Those with whom one disagrees should not be regarded as enemies but rather as people whose views deserve careful examination and may shed light on one's own.

Thomas Jefferson once said that "difference of opinion leads to inquiry, and inquiry to truth." Jefferson, a broadly educated man, argued that "if a nation expects to be ignorant and free . . . it expects what never was and never will be." As individuals and as a nation, it is imperative that we consider the opinions of others and examine them with skill and discernment. The Opposing Viewpoints Series is intended to help readers achieve this goal.

David L. Bender and Bruno Leone,
Founders

Introduction

> *"No decision in war, no military policy proposed to or considered by the Congress, no military operation—nothing in the military realm—occurs that does not derive in some way from the relationship between civilians, to whom the U.S. Constitution assigns responsibility for national defense, and the military leadership, which manages, administers, and leads the armed forces."*
>
> *—Richard H. Kohn, professor, University of North Carolina at Chapel Hill*

Western scholars generally agree that civilian control of the military is preferable to military control of the state. Indeed, scholars often view the doctrine of civilian control of the military as a staple of Western democracy. The decision to declare war, invade, or end a conflict can have such a significant impact on a nation's citizens, they reason, that such decisions are best made by those who represent the will of the people. According to history professor Richard H. Kohn in *American Diplomacy*, "the point of civilian control is to make security subordinate to the larger purposes of a nation, rather than the other way around. The purpose of the military is to defend society, not to define it." The tension created by this civil-military relationship is reflected in many armed forces controversies. In fact, the principles that shape civilian control of the military in the United States, the cultural gap between civil and military society, and the experience of civil and military leaders who have put the principles of civilian control into practice in the United States inform much of the armed forces debate.

Since the founding of the United States more than two hundred years ago, the relationship between civil society and the military organizations established to protect it has been tense. The nation's founders feared too much power placed in the hands of any individual or group. They feared large standing armies, powerful legislatures, and potent executives. Their fears—the threat to liberty posed by a sizable standing army and the danger that an unchecked legislature or executive might unnecessarily take a nation to war—are reflected in the words of James Madison, speaking before the Constitutional Convention in June 1787:

> A standing military force, with an overgrown Executive, will not long be safe companions to liberty. The means of defense against foreign danger, have been always the instruments of tyranny at home. Among the Romans it was a standing maxim to excite a war, whenever a revolt was apprehended. Throughout all Europe, the armies kept up under the pretext of defending, have enslaved the people.

The means to address these fears are manifested in the U.S. Constitution, which assigns responsibility for national defense to civilians—Congress—and establishes the president as commander in chief. The management and administration of the armed forces resides with military leadership.

For many years, the United States maintained a small standing army. Although the government built up its armed forces during times of war, after most wars, the force was quickly demobilized. The Cold War between the former Soviet Union and the United States, however, created a need for a larger peacetime military force. By 1951, in response to North Korea's invasion of South Korea, U.S. military personnel forces doubled from post–World War II levels to more than 3.2 million. The number never dropped below two million during the Cold War, which ended in 1989. These numbers did drop some over the decades that followed, and as of February 2009, a little over 1.39 million active-duty men and women served in the U.S. armed forces. The size of the U.S. military has resurrected concerns about civil-military relations.

Anxieties about the size of the U.S. armed forces center on the differences between civilian and military cultures. In *American Diplomacy* Kohn claims, "The military is among the least democratic institutions in human experience; martial customs and procedure clash by nature with individual freedom and civil liberty, the highest values in democratic societies." He explains that the military is authoritarian and hierarchical, insists on discipline and obedience, and emphasizes order and conformity. Democratic societies, on the other hand, are participatory, egalitarian, and individualistic, and tolerate disagreement and diversity. During the Cold War, scholars developed several different theories of how best to manage this cultural gap. Samuel P. Huntington asserted that the best way to deal with the tensions created by the gap between civilian and military culture was to professionalize the military. Huntington argued that military officers should be recognized as experts in the use of force. Civilian leaders would determine the objectives, and military professionals would decide on the best way to achieve these objectives. Huntington held that this strategy would mediate the tension of the gap because officers would willingly submit to civilian authority because the civilian world would look upon them as experts.

Other scholars, such as Morris Janowitz, suggested that socialization and education would better mediate the tension created by the gap between civilian and military culture. He agreed with Huntington that the military world is fundamentally conservative and more resistant to change than the less structured civilian society. Janowitz, however, countered that the better way to mediate this tension was to promote conscription, which would bring a wider variety of people to the military. Janowitz also recommended the implementation of more Reserve Officers' Training Corps (ROTC) programs in colleges. In addition, he suggested that the civilian and military elite should work together to promote standards in military education that promote the ideals and norms of civil society. These policies would better integrate both cultures, he reasoned.

While scholars continue to debate how best to mediate the gap between these two cultures, many believe that the relationship between civil and military society in the United States is unhealthy. Some have expressed concern that if the military holds civilian norms in contempt, it might question the value of defending it. Others worry that the cultural gap between civilians and the military reduces the nation's ability to maintain an effective armed force. One particular fear is that an inexperienced civilian government might, through inappropriate policies, undermine the military and thus threaten U.S. national security. These concerns are magnified when a new administration comes to office. Indeed, the level of civilian control varies, depending on the political leaders' experience and the defense needs of the nation. For the leaders of the armed forces, the election of a new administration can be unsettling. "It's like waking up in the morning, looking across the bed, and discovering you've got a new wife. You've never met her, you don't know what she wants or what she's thinking, and you have no idea what will happen when she wakes up," a four-star general explains in Richard H. Kohn's article in a 2008 issue of *World Affairs*.

Indeed, throughout U.S. history, the relationship between the nation's military and civil leaders has worked to both serve and compromise the national interest. The collaboration between President Franklin Roosevelt and his secretaries of war and navy and the heads of the two armed services is considered a model of how the relationship can serve the national interest. They kept each other informed, and Roosevelt included the military in the major allied conferences during World War II. During the Vietnam conflict, however, these relationships led to policies that did not serve the national interest. According to Kohn in *World Affairs*, "The distrust, manipulation, and absence of candor that colored relations between President Lyndon Johnson, Defense Secretary Robert McNamara, and his senior military advisors offers a case in point; to this day Robert Strange McNamara arouses hatred and contempt among military officers who were not even born when he ruled the Pentagon." In the eyes of many, poor leadership during the Vietnam War not only led to a military failure, but also so divided the nation that the heightened tensions between civil and military society continue to this day.

Decades later, the president—the commander in chief—and his advisors continue to negotiate the challenges of civilian control of the military. The goals of the founders, the theories of scholars, and the experience of those civil and military leaders who came before will surely influence the decisions of the current administration. These goals, theories, and experience also shape the views of the authors in the following chapters in *Opposing Viewpoints: The Armed Forces*: What Role Should the Armed Forces Play? Who Should Serve in the Armed Forces? How Should Armed Forces Resources Be Managed? and What Policies Best Govern Armed Forces Personnel? "Democracy," writes Professor Kohn in *American Diplomacy*, "is a disorderly form of government, often inefficient, always frustrating. Maintaining liberty and security, governing in such a manner as to achieve desirable political outcomes and at the same time military effectiveness, is among the most difficult dilemmas of human governance." The tension between civil and military society in democratic nations will likely continue—and may in fact be a necessary element of the democratic process.

OPPOSING
VIEWPOINTS®
SERIES

CHAPTER 1

What Role Should the Armed Forces Play?

Chapter Preface

Over the years a body of international law has evolved to govern war. Scholars divide the law into two areas: *jus ad bellum*, which defines the acceptable justifications for war, and *jus in bello*, which defines the acceptable use of armed force during war. By the twentieth century, a substantial body of law had formed. Nations worldwide generally agreed to these laws until the Vietnam War, following which some argued that the rules of combat should be more humane. Some analysts assert that *jus in bello*—the rules governing armed force—should be similar to the rules governing domestic law enforcement. In their eyes, humanitarian concerns should be elevated above military necessity and the national interest. In the decades following the Vietnam War, multinational conventions developed protocols to the Geneva Conventions and new interpretations of existing treaties such as the Charter of the United Nations. The United States, while involved in negotiating these treaties, chose not to ratify them. Those who agree with this decision argue that the choice was made to protect national security. Thus evolved one of several controversies in the debate over the role of armed forces—whether the United States should accept or reject strict international laws of war.

Those who advocate adherence to strict international laws of war argue that because the United States has the military prowess to win any war it fights, it should hold itself to the highest standards. Proponents do not dispute that the goal of war is to win. According to Duke University law professor Michael Byers in a 2003 article in *London Review of Books*, "Wars are fought to be won; international humanitarian law merely balances military necessity against humanitarian concerns." These commentators are concerned, however, that some modern U.S. leaders no longer see war as a high-risk, last resort solution. In fact, Byers claims that some modern leaders see war "as an attractive foreign policy option in times of domestic scandal or economic decline." U.S. military strategies that target civilians and employ inhumane weapons to further political and economic goals are immoral and run counter to American values, supporters assert. If the United States expects other nations to honor humanitarian laws of war, they reason, it must also honor them.

Opponents do not dispute the importance of balancing military necessity and humanitarian concerns. They argue, however, that the strict new international rules are based on a peacetime policing model that would limit the nation's ability to conduct war. According to attorneys David B. Rivkin Jr. and Lee A. Casey in the *National Interest*, the norms that guide peacetime law enforcement are more restrictive because the state has control. In war with another state, the state does not have the same control over the use of force. Rivkin and Casey claim, "War and peace remain different worlds, each with a unique logic and distinct imperatives that require dissimilar rules." Moreover, critics argue, the vague language of the rules open U.S. armed forces to prosecution for war crimes. Provisions of the 1977 protocols to the Geneva Conventions use terms such as doing "everything feasible," taking "all feasible precautions," or acting "to the maximum extent feasible." These terms are open-ended enough in peacetime; they become even more difficult to interpret in times of war, Rivkin and Casey reason, "where human judgment is stressed to the utmost and the fog of war reigns."

Whether the United States will accept or reject strict international rules of war designed to make the use of armed force more humane remains to be seen. The authors in the following chapter explore other controversies concerning the role armed forces should play.

| "*Extreme situations may require a pre-ventive deployment of military force.*"

Using Armed Forces Preemptively Is Sometimes Justified

Karl-Heinz Kamp

When faced with imminent threats to national security, nations once critical of U.S. foreign policy are now considering preemptive military strikes, maintains Karl-Heinz Kamp in the following viewpoint. Preemptive military actions may indeed be necessary to face modern threats, he asserts. For example, Kamp claims, states and political groups are able to attack from greater distances and proof of hostile intentions may come too late for a strike in self-defense. Thus, he reasons, an international discussion of the conditions under which preemptive military attacks may be warranted is needed. Kamp is the security policy coordinator of the Konrad Adenauer Foundation (Konrad-Adenauer-Stiftung) in Berlin.

As you read, consider the following questions:

1. According to Kamp, why was the fundamental debate over defense strategy largely ignored in Europe?

Karl-Heinz Kamp, "The New Political Reality of Pre-emptive Defence," *Canadian Military Journal*, vol. 6, Summer 2005, p. 76. Reproduced by permission.

2. In the author's view, why is making the distinction between *preemptive* and *preventive* strikes limited in practice?

3. How does the question of urgency create a dilemma when considering weapons of mass destruction, in the author's opinion?

In light of the fierce transatlantic debates of recent years, most Europeans appear to have forgotten that George W. Bush became president with the firm intention to reduce US commitments and engagements abroad. In contrast to his predecessor, he demonstrated only limited interest in the Near East and Middle East and only halfheartedly pursued President [Bill] Clinton's counterterrorism approach. Instead, Bush focused on the idea of a global missile defence, which led to the European accusation that this isolationist president intended to retreat to a "Fortress America."

A New Examination of Pre-emptive Defence

The tragedy [of the terrorist attacks] of September 11 [2001] brought exactly the opposite reaction. The US was prepared, for the sake of its own security, to change the political *status quo* in far distant regions—if necessary by military force. Moreover, in his speech to West Point [United States] Military Academy cadets in June of 2002, approximately nine months after the collapse of the World Trade Center and nine months before the war in Iraq, President Bush claimed the right of the United States to use armed force *before* an attack on its own territory occurred. A few months later, the option of pre-emptive defence was laid down in the new US National Security Strategy (NSS). Critics saw therein a breach of the prohibition on wars of aggression set down in international law, while its proponents referred to the changed threat situation. All of this makes a new examination of the concept of defence necessary.

In Europe, this fundamental debate on security policy was largely ignored. Only a few international law experts and individual politicians took notice of the explosiveness of the question. One reason for this has been, among other things, that the *general* discussion about pre-emption ignited by the American president coincided with the *specific* case of Iraq. In that sense, transatlantic dispute over Iraq precluded a sober discussion on the future interpretation of "defence." However, neither European policy makers nor the public at large will be able to avoid this complex question because the consequences transcend a purely American dimension.

What rationale lies behind the claim for pre-emptive strikes? Why is it not only an American issue but also an international reality? How can the misuse of force be avoided?

The Logic of Pre-emptive Military Force

The major reason for American support for pre-emptive strikes is the acknowledgement of a fundamentally changed threat situation, particularly after the crucial date of 11 September 2001. This does not only concern the sheer existence of nuclear, biological or chemical weapons—they do not represent a truly new factor in today's threat analysis. What is decisive, however, is the combination of three different threat elements: the spread of weapons of mass destruction, the availability of the means of delivery for them (rockets or cruise missiles) and weapon-technology progress with respect to range and accuracy. Thus, more and more states and nongovernmental organizations (NGOs) are now able to project destructive power over long distances. Geographic distance is becoming less of a factor in threat analysis. The parallel to this development is that those defending against such attacks have less and less time to react. The traditional NATO [North Atlantic Treaty Organization] principle of waiting for the proof of an opponent's intention to attack (for example, the hostile operational movement of Warsaw Pact troops) before activating military defence was valid during the Cold War, but it is becoming increasingly questionable today. Under present circumstances, the proof of an opponent's intention to attack might be the detonation of a chemical weapon in a major city. To wait for such a case, considering the potential number of casualties, would be unjustifiable. Instead, in extreme cases, it must be possible to effectively counter such threats before they become acute.

Currently, however, in American usage, the distinction between "pre-emptive" and "preventive" strikes is made—a difference that is more than a linguistic subtlety. One speaks of a *pre-emptive* strike when an attack is made on an enemy whose attack is imminent. A *preventive* strike means, however, that the attack is made solely on the assumption that offensive military action by the enemy will soon occur. While pre-emption used as defence in circumstances of an immediate danger can be quite legitimate, a preventive war that uses military means to assert a country's own interests is normally difficult to justify. In practice, however, the suitability of this distinction is limited. On one hand, these definitions are disputed. In fact, some European international law scholars use these definitions to mean exactly the opposite. On the other hand, concrete, specific dangers and scenarios, which, in any case, are to a certain degree open to interpretation, could only rarely be assigned to one of the two categories. While the state that uses military force will always present its actions as pre-emptive, the critics will generally blame the action as either preventive or simply as aggressive.

The Relevance for Europe

Regardless of the terminology, the questions of when and under what circumstances armed force may be used can no longer be ignored. Nations other than Washington [referring to Washington, D.C., the capital of the United States] have now drawn the conclusion that, in extreme situations of danger, pre-emptive military strikes can also be necessary. Countries that had recently been skeptical of pre-emption considerations, now consider this option necessary. Even France—a long-time vehement critic of "pre-emptive strikes"—has claimed the right to pre-emptive deployment of its armed forces in its new "Programmation Militaire." Russia reserves the right to pre-emption—as does Australia. Even in Japan, where military restraint is anchored in the constitution, pre-emptive strikes are being discussed at the government level.

Not only have individual governments taken up the question of pre-emption, but so have alliances and organizations. At its latest summit, held in Prague in November 2002, NATO adopted a new military concept to fight terrorism (MC 472) in which, at least implicitly, pre-emption is discussed even though, for the most part, the media did not notice this change. Although the terms "pre-emption" and "anticipatory self-defence" are not explicitly mentioned, it is clear from the entire wording of the document that NATO does not fundamentally rule out pre-emptive strikes against terrorist threats. Beyond this, the European Union has discussed the pre-emption question in the framework of a new security strategy ratified in December 2003.

Thus, the idea of pre-emptive military action is no longer, as conventional wisdom would have it, an overreaction of a single American president to the disaster of September 11. Instead, the need to redefine the understanding of defence in light of new threats is being met with ever-increasing international resonance.

The Question of International Law

Regardless of a widespread willingness to consider pre-emption, questions remain with respect to the legitimacy of pre-emptive defence under international law. Strictly interpreted, the Charter of the United Nations forbids military interventions, and grants national sovereignty highest priority.

The use of force is only legitimate for the purpose of self-defence or if mandated by the UN [United Nations] Security Council. Such a narrow interpretation, however, has steadily declined in recent years. The catch phrase "rogue states" that has been used for the last few years already breaks with the primacy of national sovereignty since it implies that by ignoring fundamental values, a country can lose its rights as a state. Furthermore, the humanitarian intervention of NATO in Kosovo contradicted the classic interpretation of the Charter. In light of the inability of the UN Security Council to agree upon military action, the Bush alliance gave priority to fighting the obvious human rights violations in the Balkans over the prohibition of the use of force and thus went to war without a Security Council mandate. In contrast to the words of the UN Charter, NATO placed higher value on the protection of human rights than on a state's protection from external intervention.

Here lies the key to the progression of international law. Instead of calling for formal rules, future actions must be more about interpretation and judgment. For each concrete situation, the fundamental values that underpin international law need to be weighed against each other. From this perspective, it is not only issues such as the danger from weapons of mass destruction or humanitarian requirements that would justify pre-emptive military intervention—it would also be conceivable, in extreme cases, to intervene to protect natural resources necessary for life. Examples might include a vital threat from ecologically irresponsible barrage projects, or dramatically unsafe nuclear power stations near an international border.

Almost inevitably, a break from a formal interpretation of international law to a discretionary and deliberative mechanism creates legal uncertainty. The decision to deploy troops, therefore, must be bound to certain concrete requirements and criteria, such as the imminence of danger, the plausibility of the threat and the proportionality of the means.

None of these criteria is precisely measurable or legally enforceable, nor is the list of conditions complete. Here, political debate must occur within individual states as well as in the United Nations in order to achieve as broad a consensus as possible as to how these threats can be adequately addressed in the coming years in light of the changed security situation. Nevertheless, such a consensus will never completely prevent the misuse of military force. The possibility that threats will be intentionally exaggerated in order to justify the use of military force against another state or a non-state protagonist cannot be ruled out. This problem, however, will not be solved by a rigid interpretation of the UN Charter. There are enough examples in the last few decades where states have attempted to justify using their military forces based upon questionable principles of legitimacy.

The Political Decision for a Pre-emptive Military Strike

In addition to the legalities involved in a pre-emptive military strike, there is the political/practical side of the issue to be considered. Under what conditions can the political decision be taken for the use of pre-emptive strikes, and how can such decisions be implemented? When is a threat pressing enough to justify a pre-emptive strike, and upon which source (or sources) of information will the decision be made?

A pre-emptive action does not only have to entail overthrowing a government. The spectrum of possible options is, in fact, substantially broader. Nonmilitary as well as "semi-military" actions are just as conceivable against governments and nongovernmental actors. These can take place on a state's soil, or, for instance, in international waters. They can include interrupting information streams, capturing ships, intercepting aircraft, comprehensive blockading or acts of sabotage.

A History of Pre-emption

The First World War . . . was a pre-emptive war from the American point of view. America did not enter the war because it was attacked (it wasn't), nor did Germany declare war on the United States. For three years Americans had watched the war from the sidelines. It was a European conflict in which America had had no national stake. Then, in 1917, the United States decided to go to war to prevent a German victory, claiming that its goal was "to make the world safe for democracy." The second war with Germany was different, but only slightly. The very same people who now claim to oppose pre-emption have long faulted the United States for remaining neutral during the Spanish Civil War of the 1930s. If fascism had been defeated in Spain, they argue, there might not have been a Second World War at all.

David Horowitz,
"The Doctrine of Pre-emption: A Strategy of Realism,"
FrontPage Magazine, *April 15, 2003. www.frontpagemag.com.*

They can be accomplished by regular armed forces, by special forces or by secret services. The targets of pre-emptive action can be production or storage facilities for weapons of mass destruction, command centres for terrorist organizations, or various other state facilities. Each of these options has different levels of acceptability and feasibility. Destruction of a terrorist training camp is more likely to meet with public approval, on both the national and international level, than the overthrow of a government.

All of these actions have in common that they can only be justified in cases where the threat is exceedingly urgent and immediate. The question of urgency, however, leads to a serious dilemma in following this line of reasoning when considering weapons of mass destruction. If one decides as late as possible for a military strike, in order to demonstrate that the threat was obviously and without doubt imminent, the success of a countering action may potentially be much less. The attacker will by then have most likely fully developed his weapon arsenal and protected it by dispersal or by deployment in hardened underground facilities. In extreme cases, fighting the threat can be almost impossible by the time the seriousness of the situation is recognized and acknowledged. If, instead, a threat is dealt with promptly, the chances of success are usually better. On the negative side of this scenario, however, is that in such cases it would be far more difficult to demonstrate urgency and thus to receive public support.

Defining Urgency

With regard to this dilemma, it appears difficult to find a mutually acceptable definition of urgency. In the 1970s, there was already debate in America over "just" and "unjust" wars and whether an "imminent attack" was the necessary legal standard for military action, or if a "sufficient threat" might be more appropriate. Even if such a limitation must remain vague, certain criteria can nevertheless be established:

- The opponent's intention to inflict harm must be evident: for example, a head of state or a head of a terrorist group declaring such intent.

- Preparations and relevant measures to realize this intention must be recognizable, such as, the offensive relocation of troops or launch preparations for missiles. Technological developments play a large role here. If the range capability of rockets increases and allows for even shorter reaction time on the part of the potential victim, the threshold is thereby reduced at which preparation for an attack can be tolerated.

- It must be obvious that non-action dramatically increases the risks or makes later reactions almost impossible. An example of this was Israel's bombing of an Iraqi nuclear reactor in 1981. Israel asserted that the reactor would be used to make material for Iraq's nuclear weapons program. June was specified as the time for the attack because the facility was to be loaded with nuclear fuel the following month. Bombing a reactor filled with radioactive material would hardly have been possible.

With respect to each of these criteria, the question arises as to the source of the information for evaluating the danger. As a rule, the information is provided by intelligence services. To achieve an appropriate picture of the situation, not only must the available threat potential (such as weapons and military forces) be correctly portrayed, the intentions and the "strategic culture" of the opponent must be adequately rendered as well. Is there a real intention to attack? Could weapons of mass destruction be given to a third party, i.e., terrorist groups? How will the opponent react to a pre-emptive strike? At the same time, decision makers can be confronted as much with the problem of an overload of information as with a lack of reliable data. Just before the attacks of 11 September 2001, the American intelligence services experienced a flood of individual indications of a terrorist threat, many containing decisive clues. The opposite is the case for such isolated countries as North Korea. Here, the problem is one of spotty intelligence, which greatly increases the difficulty for political decision making. In both cases, the challenge lies in selecting and interpreting the available information, remembering that a degree of uncertainty in the findings is inevitable.

How difficult such an undertaking is in practice was demonstrated during the latest Iraq crisis. Although the United States possesses the most advanced information capabilities, and although Iraq was an easy intelligence target, due to international inspections over the years, no definitive picture of Iraqi weapons of mass destruction capabilities has yet been drawn.

A Necessary Debate

Extreme situations may require a preventive deployment of military force. This must then be bound to concrete conditions. None of the mentioned criteria, however, can be categorically defined or legally enforced. Moreover, this list of legal and political prerequisites for pre-emptive strikes is not complete. A debate must take place within individual countries and within the United Nations to achieve the widest possible consensus on addressing future security challenges. A public discussion is essential to prevent the abuse of pre-emptive military strikes. Even if criteria are specified for pre-emptive military deployment, the legitimacy and commensurability of such an action will always be subject to interpretation. Misuse of force cannot be excluded in principle. When political decision makers (at least, in democratic countries) have to justify their actions to a critical and informed public and must accept the consequences of bad decisions, this acts as a deterrent to the cavalier use of military might. If the public, however, declines to engage in such a debate, it gives up a substantial instrument of control over its government.

| "Unprovoked invasion is wrong no matter what ends are invoked and no matter whether the public and its elected officials unanimously agree on it."

Using Armed Forces Preemptively Is Never Justified

Michael S. Rozeff

Absolutely nothing justifies an unprovoked invasion of another country, argues Michael S. Rozeff in the following viewpoint. When one state uses its military to attack another state, innocent, blameless civilians suffer, he claims. A state has no right to act as judge and executioner, even if those running the attacked state commit evil acts, Rozeff maintains. Preemptive attacks, he reasons, punish all who get in the way, even citizens who are not guilty. The fact that the majority in a democracy believe that unprovoked attacks are in some cases justified is not enough to justify preemptive war. Rozeff is a professor of finance at the University of Buffalo.

As you read, consider the following questions:

1. How does Rozeff see the public when it is not constrained by ethics, law, or custom?

Michael S. Rozeff, "Public Opinion, Sovereignty, and Preemptive War," LewRockwell.com, May 12, 2006. Copyright © 2006 LewRockwell.com. Reproduced by permission of the publisher and the author.

2. In the author's opinion, the *National Strategy for Victory in Iraq* is an admission of what?

3. Why does the author think it is necessary to distinguish states from countries?

Defenders of democracy argue that its leaders are responsive to public opinion, or at least more responsive than under other forms of government. [Influential American writer H.L.] Mencken put it this way: "Democracy is the theory that the common people know what they want and deserve to get it good and hard." [Abraham] Lincoln viewed democracy as "that government of the people, by the people, for the people."

The obvious problem with democracy or government by public opinion is that it is still government. There is nothing sacred about public opinion or the will of a majority or all of the people. Whether or not the crowd is smart, dumb, fickle, or possessed of innate good sense is irrelevant. The main point is that the public is just as authoritarian as any dictator if its will and actions are not strongly constrained by ethics, constitution, common sense, (real) law, or custom. They are usually not so constrained. In today's democracies, the public roams over public policies, picking and choosing its next targets for regulation and regimentation. Public opinion becomes another term for tyranny and the suppression of individual freedom. Authoritarian democracy oppresses and harms many, including members of that group we call the public, as if we knew what the term meant.

The Role of Public Opinion

Democracy is a kind of protoplasm with its component parts symbiotically related: the public, its elected leaders, the media, and special interest groups representing business, labor, agriculture, technology, education, health, etc. They flow together in a fluid of money, influence, and information to produce "laws," the official acts, policies, judgments, and regulations that bind and constrain us peons who have made our will felt through this mysterious public opinion and an occasional ballot, essay, cracker-barrel conversation, or letter to an editor.

Causality is multidirectional, running from the public to its leaders and from the leaders to the public, running from lobbyists and string-pullers to politicians and back again, running every which way. But public opinion has its role. There is no doubt of that. Votes are taken and ballots counted, although sometimes too few and sometimes too many. Public opinion had something to do with ending the Vietnam War, although even after the peak of its expression that conflict continued and expanded for several years under President [Richard] Nixon. At the same time, small ruling groups influence events out of all proportion to their size. The Committee of Public Safety, a twelve-man body under [Georges] Danton and then [Maximilien] Robespierre and the Jacobins, ruled France between 1793 and 1795, not the elected Convention. No one today doubts the enormous power of the U.S. presidency, even as the president heeds public opinion.

The Pragmatic Public Wants Victory

Elected officials care enough about public opinion to go to great lengths to sound it out. In many instances, their goal is to influence opinion. They listen to the public's thoughts only in order to play back to them the songs that the public wants to hear. One such song is "victory." Dr. Peter D. Feaver helped conceive and draft a White House document (released in November 2005) titled *National Strategy for Victory in Iraq* after he had analyzed U.S. public opinion and discovered that the public would support the war if it thought that victory could be achieved. The following month the president [George W. Bush] made a speech at the [U.S.] Naval Academy in which he used the word victory 15 times.

The pragmatic public wants victory at the moment [May 2006] (or wanted it six months ago). The president wants victory and promises it. None of this wanting, promising, fighting and warring makes them right. In fact there is nothing right about it. The sovereignty of the public, or the public joined to its assembled officials, or the elected officials influencing the public, or of our democracy—none of it has legitimacy. Whether or not the U.S. Constitution was ever legitimate, we cannot legitimately manufacture or make up rules as we go along. That is, we cannot justifiably break those fundamentally right, sound, and virtually self-evident rules we should be following and replace them with "laws" we declare are right.

Unprovoked Invasion Is Wrong

As Americans who promulgate the rights of man, we are supposed to know we shouldn't invade another country simply because it suits our purposes. It seems that many of us do not know this. It seems that many others of us who do know this willfully and evilly ignore it. No matter what public opinion says, it cannot be right to invade Iraq, wrecking the country and killing innocent people. It cannot be right to do this in order to remove their leaders, or in order to deprive third-party terrorists of shelter, or in order to keep terrorists on the run, or in order to deliver a decisive blow to an ideology. Yet these are the precise reasons given for the invasion of Iraq by our leaders in the *National Strategy for Victory in Iraq*. This document is an open admission of national wrong by standards of traditional justice and by the standards of American ideals. Unprovoked invasion is wrong no matter what ends are invoked and no matter whether the public and its elected officials unanimously agree on it. We will pay for these crimes.

Even had unused weapons of mass destruction (whatever they are) been located inside Iraq, even if truckloads of unused chemical gas had found their way into Syria, even if shells tainted with anthrax or mustard gas had been found, none of these would have justified an unprovoked invasion either, whether the United Nations [UN] said so or not. The UN no more than any other political body has the legitimacy to make up any laws it chooses.

Why Invasion Is Ethically Wrong

The ethical right and wrong of aggressive warfare among states are not hard to understand. This is so even if we recognize that states are evil or illegitimate organizations and even if we believe that it is fitting and proper to undermine them or see them fall.

One must first distinguish a state from a country. A state is typically a small organization of leaders. They control the military. They collect taxes. They make rules and regulations. The country consists of large numbers of people ruled by the state. The states have the armed forces and the weapons.

One state does not aggress against another state if its armed forces and weapons are employed in defense of its country and employed *properly*, for example, without undifferentiated attacks upon civilians. However, it is wrong for one state to initiate an attack upon another state. For example, it is surely wrong if a state attacks other states because the latter are thought to possess weapons, or thought to have a desire to obtain weapons, or thought to be possible threats, or thought to possess a critical resource like oil, or thought to be enriching uranium. It is also wrong to make an unprovoked attack in order to free the attacked state's people.

Here are a few ethical reasons why such unprovoked attacks are wrong. Ethicists and jurists versed in the nature of the just war may have further arguments.

Harming innocent civilians. When one state attacks another, it attacks both a country and a state. The country's civilians are harmed, often terminally. Since these civilians have not attacked or harmed the attacking state, the attacker has no just cause to attack them. They are relatively innocent even if their state is relatively guilty of some crimes.

No self-defense justification. The attacked state has not attacked or made war against its attacker. It basically hasn't done anything to the attacking state. The attacked state's weapons are not bad in and of themselves and therefore are not harming the attackers. The bad would be in using these weapons wrongly against the attacker, but this has not happened. There is no self-defense justification for an unprovoked attack.

Lack of due process. An attacking state has no right to act as judge, jury, and executioner of another state, even if that state has evil people running it who have committed evil acts (and what state hasn't?). Evil deeds are properly assessed according to the degree of what has been done by impartial bodies. Then the remedies should fit the crimes.

There are no such impartial bodies in the world, but this remains the ideal that we can reason from. This ideal suggests that an attacking state that already has dirty hands (because it *is* a state) can't even pretend to play this role. It suggests that the people of the country being attacked have a better claim to bring down their state than another state does. It also suggests another possibility, that one or more external bodies constitute themselves (free of all existing states) with the aim of hearing evidence and judging the actions of existing states. These would be "shadow" international courts of justice. Even if they possessed no punitive powers, they could be influential.

Lack of appropriate remedies. An attacker who starts a war imposes indiscriminate and bloody remedies, basically punishments, upon all who get in its way, guilty and guiltless alike, no matter what the degree of guilt. Even if the U.S. had a right to bring down Iraq's state, the just methods are not those of war on a broad scale. They are not even necessarily punishment of the members of the state. That imposes the current made-in-the-U.S.A. brand of dealing with crimes.

The Supreme Crime

Preventive war is, very simply, the "supreme crime" condemned at [the International Military Tribunal at] Nuremberg [following World War II].

That was understood by those with some concern for their country. As the US invaded Iraq, historian Arthur Schlesinger wrote that [George W.] Bush's grand strategy is "alarmingly similar to the policy that imperial Japan employed at Pearl Harbor, on a date which, as an earlier American president said it would, lives in infamy." FDR [Franklin Delano Roosevelt] was right, he added, "but today it is we Americans who live in infamy." It is no surprise that "the global wave of sympathy that engulfed the United States after 9/11 [2001 terrorist attacks] has given way to a global wave of hatred of American arrogance and militarism," and the belief that Bush is "a greater threat to peace than [former Iraqi president] Saddam Hussein."

Noam Chomsky,
"Preventive War 'the Supreme Crime,'"
Z Net, August 11, 2003. www.zmag.org.

Such a method rules out restitution approaches that place the victim's interests above those of states.

No right to preempt actions of the country's people. An attacker has no right to override the actions (including doing nothing) of the state's people who are living under that state. It has no right either to impose an alternative authority on those people or to alter their situation in ways that they may not approve of. Doing so violates that people's rights. For example, if the people had one voice, they might be content to wait out their current rulers and hope for better under the next ones. They might be content under the present ruler because they fear a neighboring state will absorb them if that ruler is deposed. The people might be unhappy. They might even welcome being freed if they knew they'd be better off afterwards. But they may not know or even expect that they would be better off. They might fear a war-ravaged country. The people might prefer the existing certainty to the uncertainty of a new situation. If they can't foresee the outcome of being freed by an interloping attacker, they might calculate that the uncertainty of being freed by another state makes them worse off despite their currently undesirable condition.

No right to trespass. The people of a country might love their lands and country so much that they don't want to see foreigners trespassing on their lands and property. They might even believe that they have a right that their property not be destroyed or trespassed. In fact, they might even begin to defend themselves and their property against foreign "saviors."

Meanwhile a paternalistic attack to free a people presumes that the attacker knows that it can improve the utility of the people in the attacked state. But since an attacker can't know this or even measure it, it can't ever justify the attack.

Who's Responsible?

If a state's aggressions are sometimes held in check by the public, this is good. Even Franklin Roosevelt had to drag the U.S. into war against the Empire of Japan. If the public urges its officials into war as by Remembering the *Maine*,[1] this is bad. Democracy, being the protoplasm that it is, makes it hard at times to assign responsibility. Usually we can tell. Usually our leaders bear the lion's share of the responsibility. [Harry S.] Truman launched the U.S. into the Korean "police action." [John F.] Kennedy and [Lyndon B.] Johnson (with the

1. On February 15, 1898, the USS *Maine* exploded and sank, precipitating the Spanish-American War and popularizing the phrase "Remember the Maine." The cause of the explosion remains a mystery.

Congress) heavily raised the ante in Vietnam. [Ronald] Reagan went into Grenada. Bush I's [George H.W. Bush's] inept diplomacy catalyzed the Persian Gulf War, and he orchestrated the coalition campaign. [Bill] Clinton bombed Iraq and Yugoslavia and sent troops into Haiti and Somalia. It is the Congress right now that has sanctioned Iran for years and continues to apply pressure in conjunction with the president and his agents. Bush II [George W. Bush] without doubt brought about the current Iraq War.

For the most part, the responsibility for America's warfare rests primarily with the state and only secondarily with the population. The leaders pull the people along in one way or another.

The Public Changes Its Mind

If the public wants wrong and its elected officials want wrong, then they shall have wrong. All their laws and words shall not make it right. If the public and/or its officials declare that Iran shall not enrich uranium and pass a law to that effect, a law that results in war with Iran, nothing shall make it right. It will be everlastingly wrong.

And when the public decides it wants right, it may be able to get its way. Then again it may not. Maybe the public will change its mind and turn against the president. His popularity keeps sinking. Maybe the public wants to hear a new tune on its political iPod, a peace ditty. When and if this happens, my happiness over the event will be quite limited because I will know that nothing fundamental has changed. The public will be thinking in pragmatic terms, calculating that "it isn't worth it." And if they thought it were worth it, if they thought victory were attainable, then would invasion be right? If so, we had no reason to complain when the Germans attacked Poland in 1939. They won, at least temporarily, didn't they? Might makes right, doesn't it?

The public and/or its elected officials still think they are the sovereign creators of right and wrong. They still think that they can make up almost any rule they want to and make it law, and that this confers legitimacy upon their wishes. They still believe in democracy, in public opinion.

So if they change their minds, this democracy of ours will still be authoritarian. The time bombs of oppression will still be ticking away, and I will still be wishing for a great many of us to come to our senses and relearn the meaning of law and restraint, hopefully without the "benefit" of a democracy hanging around our necks.

> "The United States performs nation-building activities to establish conditions that further our national interests."

Armed Forces Are Necessary for Nation Building

Gregory L. Cantwell

The U.S. government should ask the military to perform nation-building activities when its leaders determine that such activities will protect national interests, claims Gregory L. Cantwell in the following viewpoint. In fact, the U.S. military has historically helped build governments and restore stability following regime changes. Coordinating the diverse organizations that must work together to build nations is challenging, but it's a role for which the military is well equipped, Cantwell contends. Since adequate resources to complete these operations are necessary, public support for nation-building operations is critical, he reasons. Cantwell is a U.S. Army strategic plans and policy officer.

Gregory L. Cantwell, "Nation-Building: A Joint Enterprise," *Parameters*, vol. 37, Autumn 2007, pp. 54–61, 67. Copyright © 2007 U.S. Army War College. Reproduced by permission.

As you read, consider the following questions:

1. Despite the fact that the military has no control of national power, for what does Cantwell claim the military is often held accountable?

2. What language in DoD Directive 3000.05 identifies nation building as a core military mission?

3. In the author's view, what are some of the factors that complicate achieving unity of effort in nation-building operations?

Consider the following questions. The Army is at war, but is the nation at war? Has the nation sufficiently mobilized the elements of national power in support of a global war effort? Have average Americans changed their lives because of the war? Is popular support for the war in Iraq high enough to mobilize the nation? Public opinion polls in January 2007 showed that support for President [George W.] Bush's handling of the war was at an all-time low of 26 percent. Similar polls suggested that 54 percent of the American public believed that the United States was losing the war in Iraq. Then Chief of Staff of the Army, General Peter Schoomaker, began his remarks to the House Armed Services Committee on 27 June 2006 with these words.

> America's Army remains at war. And we will be fighting this war for the foreseeable future. This is not just the Army's war. Yet in light of the scale of our commitment we bear the majority of the burden, serving side by side with Marines and our other sister services and coalition partners.

General Schoomaker identified the crux of the issue; America relies upon the Army, and from a joint perspective, the Department of Defense [DoD] to fight and win the nation's wars. The American people have every expectation that the military will succeed when committed. They hold the military accountable for achieving victory. Yet the military does not command or control the elements of national power (diplomatic, information, and economic) essential for achieving victory.

Intellectuals argue that wars are won or lost by nations and not by militaries. The military does, however, make a significant contribution to any eventual outcome of a conflict. Many observers believe the military is responsible for the final outcome of any conflict despite a multitude of related factors. For example, there are those who contend that America lost the war in Vietnam even though, from a tactical standpoint, the Army did not lose a battle. Many blamed this loss on the lack of a coordinated national strategy, but continue to hold the military accountable for failing to develop a winning strategy. Similarly, in Iraq, many claim the war is being lost and blame the leadership of the Department of Defense for any number of strategic errors. This harkens back to the issue that the military is accountable to fight and win America's wars.

Furthering National Interests

Others question why the military needs to support such missions as nation-building. The fact of the matter is the military as an element of national power is employed to protect the United States' national interests. The military is exercising that role in Iraq because national leaders believe that critical interests are at stake. The United States performs nation-building activities to establish conditions that further our national interests. There are a number of countries needing assistance with nation-building, but the military is not capable of providing direct assistance to all in need. The nation's leaders apparently do not consider national interests sufficient to warrant military deployments to all of these regions. Africa has a predominance of the poorest nations in the world. Genocide, famine, disease, and failed governments are often cited as sufficient justification for the US military's nation-building assistance. Yet, because vital national security interests are not at stake, the military is not substantially engaged throughout Africa. It goes without saying that the world has more needs than the United States has the capacity to provide solutions. National interests serve to prioritize the employment of America's military.

A pragmatic approach might suggest that the military take the lead in developing the capabilities needed to succeed across the spectrum of conflict, even if those capabilities exist in the other elements of national power. The American military has already adopted numerous measures to enhance its capabilities in time of war and is transforming and reorganizing itself to meet the realities of today's global environment. . . .

Answering the Counterargument

The counterargument to this approach is that the military needs to concentrate exclusively on its warfighting capabilities that are not found in the other elements of national power. Keeping the armed forces strictly focused on combat missions appeals to those who dislike a large standing military and the associated expense. It may be more cost-effective, however, if the American military integrates the organic capabilities required for nation-building. Such capabilities would be of major importance at the conclusion of military operations. In fact, history is replete with examples of the US military performing post-conflict operations, to include building government capacity following regime change. The Iraq conflict is not the first theater where the military has faced the challenges of nation-building, reconstruction, or counterinsurgency operations.

The debate related to the missions of the military centers on the role played by the Department of Defense in achieving national security objectives. The nation tries to maintain a balance between the missions assigned to the military and the resources allocated. Equally as important is the need to maintain a balance between authority and responsibility. Military

Combining Hard and Soft Power

The United States should promote greater coordination between the military and civilian agencies, especially in the context of counterinsurgency and nation-building efforts. A promising model is the Provincial Reconstruction Team, first used in Afghanistan, in which a small military contingent works closely with civilian experts and host government representatives to encourage governance, provide security, and deliver targeted assistance to a local population. Going forward, the military should formalize this cooperation, encouraging the development of units tasked for nation-building and advisory missions in which there is a dedicated civilian contribution. By combining hard and soft power, the United States can maintain its influence despite constraints on available resources.

Paul K. MacDonald,
"Rebalancing American Foreign Policy,"
Dædalus, Spring 2009.

professionals are important participants in this debate. . . . The Department of Defense should establish joint nation-building organizations, leverage existing initiatives, and establish regional training centers—designed to rapidly improve the nation's ability to perform SSTR [stability, security, transition, and reconstruction] operations.

Executive Authority

The president has significant latitude in determining how to develop and execute foreign policy. Article II of the United States Constitution establishes the president as the commander in chief of the armed forces and gives him broad authority in international affairs. Congress established the National Security Council in the executive office of the president with the implementation of the National Security Act of 1947. The president organizes the cabinet to best accomplish his agenda. Presidential directives are issued in an effort to establish the structure and authorities needed to enact the administration's priorities. . . .

DoD Directive 3000.05, *Military Support for Stability, Security, Transition, and Reconstruction (SSTR) Operations*, dated 28 November 2005, outlines SSTR operations as core military missions. It further directs the Department of Defense to include plans for SSTR operations in all its military planning. The following excerpt illustrates the meaning of this directive.

> Many stability operations tasks are best performed by indigenous, foreign or U.S. civilian professionals. Nonetheless, U.S. military forces shall be prepared to perform all tasks necessary to establish or maintain order when civilians cannot do so.

Many of the tasks addressed in the directive call for the development of representative governments; rebuilding indigenous institutions to include various security forces, correctional facilities, and judicial systems; reviving private sector economic activity; and constructing necessary infrastructure. These tasks are all part of nation-building. The intent of this directive is to ensure the Department of Defense has the capabilities required to succeed in SSTR operations without the immediate assistance from other agencies. The directive clarifies a debate within the military on whether nation-building should be a core task. It does not, however, provide any of the resources required to accomplish this type of mission.

Facilitating Crucial Coordination

Joint doctrine is authoritative within the military. Joint Publication 3-08, *Interagency, Intergovernmental Organization, and Nongovernmental Organization Coordination During Joint Op-*

erations, establishes the fundamental principles to facilitate coordination between the Department of Defense and other agencies. This document advances the discussion of the challenges facing the military and the joint task force commander in achieving "unity of effort" in coordinating the elements of national power. . . .

However, these relationships often can create challenges leading back to the initial issue of balance between authority and responsibility.

Several factors complicate achieving unity of effort [in nation-building activities]. First, unity of effort is convoluted by the diversity of organizations that require synchronization. Representatives of these organizations need to have the authority to make policy decisions that channel their resources in a common direction. The authority over such resources is often fragmented among different departments in any bureaucratic organization. . . .

Second, the scope of the mission further obscures synchronization of efforts. The challenge of reestablishing order to facilitate civilian authority is complex, vast, and difficult to quantify. For example, the area in Iraq is inhabited by more than 27 million people who have historical ethnic and religious clashes that may be irreconcilable. No organization, other than the military, has the equipment, personnel, and resources to address a problem this complex. . . .

Third, theater [field of operations] diversity inhibits unity of effort. Theater diversity prevents the combatant commander from developing standard solutions. Standard solutions facilitate unity of effort if they are applied throughout the region. Programs that are successful in one province or district may not be effective in another area. Many theaters have non-homogeneous populations that create unique regional challenges. The combination of these factors makes it difficult to centrally control an approach that requires near-unique solutions. This diversity complicates unity of effort by placing a premium on situational awareness at the local level, even down to the village level, in an effort to determine effective actions. Many organizations lack the broad regional focus of a geographic combatant commander. The Department of State, for example, organizes by country rather than by region. These factors suggest the military is best suited for a comprehensive approach if unity of effort is to be achieved.

The Leading Agency for Nation-Building

The military has a clear requirement to prepare for the conduct of nation-building tasks. The debate does continue, however, over whether the military should be the lead agency for all operations or just those associated with conflict. Since the military is required to perform across the spectrum of conflict, the result of this debate is largely inconsequential. The military must have the capability to perform SSTR operations on a global basis. Other organizations can augment these capabilities, relieve the military of tasks as the situation matures, or be the lead agency for coordination. These organizations will, however, continue to rely upon the military for the mission of restoring stability. . . .

The Department of Defense is the best agency to lead the coordination of the elements of national power for stability, security, transition, and reconstruction operations. Faced with the reconstruction of Europe in 1949 Winston Churchill stated, "It is quite impossible to draw any precise line between military and nonmilitary problems." Similarly, today's nation-building challenges require an integration of all the elements of power, civil and military. Embracing this reality will enhance DoD's chances of success. The Department of Defense should leverage each of the geographic combatant commander's regional power bases to integrate all the elements of national power, while providing a sound foundation for future military operations. Further, there is value in ensuring that the national security debate includes an understanding of the military resources necessary to defend the nation. Finally, America needs to be committed to efforts to fully resource the critical coordination elements required for SSTR operations.

> "If the government wants to nation build, employ people who are trained in economics and engineering, rather than people trained in the wedge formation and the hasty ambush."

Armed Forces Should Not Be Responsible for Nation Building

Peter Allen

U.S. armed forces should stick to their primary mission, asserts Peter Allen in the following viewpoint. Remaining the best fighting force in the world is difficult, however, when international organizations hold militaries to unrealistic human rights standards, he claims. Moreover, Allen argues, the government is asking U.S. soldiers to set up stable governments, even though soldiers are not trained to do so. If the U.S. government wants to build nations, he reasons, it should hire economists and engineers and let soldiers return to what they do best. Allen is a government official working abroad.

As you read, consider the following questions:

1. According to Allen, how do Americans see their army?

Peter Allen, "Warfare, Workfare, and Nation Building," *Liberty*, vol. 22, November 1, 2008, pp. 31–38. Copyright © 2008 Liberty Foundation. Reproduced by permission.

2. What can one civilian death jeopardize, in the author's opinion?

3. In the author's view, what is the U.S. Army's most important obligation, as dictated by the Constitution?

Ask most Americans about the track record of their army and they will tell you proudly that it has never lost a war. Despite the result in Vietnam—where, many people will tell you, we did not lose; we just stopped playing after losing interest—Americans see their army as an invincible force, feared and respected all over the world.

Yet, as we continue to fight in Iraq and Afghanistan, it is clear that the force that won the world wars of the 20th century needs a makeover, and soon. The U.S. Army has grown haphazardly out of control and is so far removed from its original mission that chaos is the only possible result.

The Army is proud of its roots, and rightly so. It is older than the nation itself, tracing its roots to June 14, 1775, a full year before the signing of the Declaration of Independence. Whenever there has been a crisis, throughout the nation's history, the Army has been there to help out—for better or for worse. Whether it was fighting off the British a second time in 1812, or subjugating the native population on the frontier, the Army was there. Afterwards, the Army, which had anticolonialism at its roots, was often a force of liberation for foreign peoples.

A New World

But a funny thing happened on the way to self-congratulation. After defeating the Axis powers in WWII [World War II] and facing the threat of the Soviet Union, the Army had to deal with a new world of urban fighting and microscopic inspection of casualties. A bevy of international organizations such as the UN [United Nations], IMF [International Monetary Fund], World Bank, and Amnesty International, just to name a few, now hold any military operation to an unprecedented human rights standard. While in the past the U.S. Army was respected for the military results it produced, now one civilian death can be enough to jeopardize an operation that, in theory, might free millions of people from oppression.

Once, dictators could commit any number of atrocities and be fairly sure that word would be so late in reaching potential opponents that the deed would already be done and accountability would be impossible. [Adolf] Hitler is said to have asked his commanders when they expressed concern over what the consequences would be of his order to exterminate all Poles who stood in his way, "Who remembers the Armenians?" History had taught him to be heedless of the outrage of the world community.

Today, fortunately, the fate of the Armenians could not go unnoticed. The rich nations of the world have not yet proven able to stop genocide from happening; but the international spotlight has made it nearly impossible to hide this or other atrocities. Everyone knew what was going on in Kosovo and Rwanda while it was going on, and the outrage over Darfur [Sudanese genocide] would not be possible without our modern technology and watchdog agencies.

Couple these facts of the contemporary world with the unquestioned strength of the U.S. military and its invincibility in any conventional war and you begin to understand the current controversies.

Today, the Army has to balance a bewildering array of tasks that range from its traditional mission of protecting the nation from international threats, to rebuilding shattered nations, to providing health care, education, and recreation to the families of its members.

A Workfare Military

To understand what has happened, it is important to realize that the Army now is as much a workfare program as it is anything else. I refer not to the average income of those who join its ranks, but rather to the Army's provision of a social safety net for people who are not sure what to do with their lives, or who have goals—other than protecting the country— that Army enlistment can help them attain.

If you are feeling unsure about your future, dislike your job, have a pregnant girlfriend, desire U.S. citizenship, or despise school so much that you will do *any*thing to get your parents to stop asking you about college, then you can join the Army. After doing so you will have a taxpayer-funded job, the credibility imparted by an organization with a storied history, and the ego boost of hearing millions of people thanking you for your "selfless sacrifice for our country." It doesn't matter that you may not have any idea what it truly means to serve in the Army. You are now part of something larger than yourself, and that's enough.

Because the Army has set itself up as a workfare program, and because those at the top of the organization have a vested interest in keeping their budget large, in the neighborhood of $420 billion at latest count, there is no incentive to make real cuts or shift the mission. The inevitable truth about government agencies remains unchallenged—they can only get bigger. Our military accounts for 43% of the entire world's military spending, and eats up over 20% of our own budget.

New Roles for Soldiers

This prompts a number of questions. Just what is a bigger Army doing? Is it doing those things well? Could someone else do them better?

To answer the first question, let's look at the tasks now being undertaken by the U.S. Army in Iraq and Afghanistan. Despite campaign pledges to the contrary, the [George W.] Bush administration is now [in late 2008] fully involved in nation building. It became clear long ago (and by long ago I mean in the 19th century, with the experiences of the European colonial powers, not within the last couple of years in Iraq) that combat operations are not going to bring peace and stability to the third world. Prosperity will come to these nations only when locals reach the point where they can provide their own security.

A change in foreign policy that recognizes this fact was necessary. To that end we started using our soldiers like Peace Corps volunteers. Handing out flyers, giving candy to children, spreading goodwill, and teaching the locals how to provide basic medical and veterinary care are now part of the job. Never mind that at Fort Benning's Sand Hill you were taught the basics of the wedge formation, how to conduct a hasty ambush, and other more properly military skills. Now you will be handed a card with extremely restrictive rules of engagement, and told not to look at the women in the village while your commander attends a shura [consultation] in which the local leaders complain about how their generator no longer works. Soon after this meeting, however, you will be called to the site of an IED [improvised explosive device] where you will be required to shoot at someone who may well be a member of the family to whom, at the shura, you swore you meant no harm. Your unit will also be supplemented with "civil-military operations" units that will pass out money for building projects, and "psychological operations" units that will make colorful flyers depicting smiling locals receiving a free prayer rug for agreeing to stop shooting at coalition forces.

During the 15 months in which your unit is deployed, pending a phone call that increases that duration, a contingent of uniformed soldiers will remain at your home station. Some are injured and cannot deploy; others just got selected to remain behind. These soldiers will look after the garrison and provide needed support to the deployed unit, but inevitably they will also answer questions from lonely family members about who is going to mow their lawns, now that the husband is gone.

This additional force is, nowadays, just as important as the force actually deployed; assisting families is the next closest thing to combat duty.

All of this started benignly enough. Families have always come together to cope with the stresses of war and wartime. Now, however, managing this stress has become a central military function, performed by uniformed soldiers.

Is the military performing its nonmilitary functions well? Could someone else do them better? The answers are "No" and "Yes."

Handing Foreign Policy to the Military

First and foremost, the military is a fighting organization. Soldiers are recruited and trained to fight wars. This is the Army's most important obligation and the one dictated by the Constitution. The Army is supposed to be an institution that provides physical security. The U.S. has always maintained that the military is a tool of the government and does not make policy or political decisions, but the truth on the ground is quite different.

In her book *The Punishment of Virtue*, Sarah Chayes, former NPR [National Public Radio] correspondent turned resident of Kandahar [or Qandahar, Afghanistan], talks about her dealings with the U.S. representation in Afghanistan. For every State Department representative she meets, there are thousands of military personnel. The military rank and file are the ones the locals see and deal with most. The U.S. military is the de facto foreign policy maker in the area. It is the effects of its decisions that the people most feel; it is military uniforms that the people most often see. By creating a military that is simultaneously an armed force, a workfare program, and a diplomatic enterprise, we have handed the reins of our foreign policy over to the leaders of the military.

A Bad Idea

We now rely by default on the U.S. military to deal with everything from humanitarian crisis intervention to large-scale reconstruction efforts in failing states and post-conflict environments.

Relying on the U.S. military to master such tasks was always a bad idea, for three basic reasons. First, the U.S. military lacks both the organizational culture and particular expertise for the governance and economic tasks involved in state- and nation-building. Second, when civilian authority makes the military do such things anyway, it causes U.S. foreign policy as a whole to project a military optic that is often counterproductive—particularly in missions that depend on partnerships with nongovernmental organizations, international organizations, the private sector and civilian populations. Third, the military's default operation of peace and stability operations tends to suck all the oxygen out of the room, demobilizing the government's sense of urgency to put in place truly appropriate capabilities.

A. Heather Coyne,
"Amateur Hour: Nation-Building in Iraq,"
American Interest, *November-December 2007.*

The Department of Defense and the Department of State have been at odds for so long that their strife is taken for granted.

One of the latest tussles, between former Defense Secretary [Donald] Rumsfeld and Secretaries of State [Colin] Powell and [Condoleezza] Rice, is just the most recent spasm. But as the military fails yet again to set up stable governments in third world countries, meanwhile cracking under the stress of constant deployments, it is time to reassess exactly what we are asking it to do.

A Return to the Army's Actual Mission

I suggest a reversion to the actual mission of the Army. Take away the civil-military affairs units—and take the Psychological Operations units along with them. If the government wants to nation build, employ people who are trained in economics and engineering, rather than people trained in the wedge formation and the hasty ambush. If you want to do information operations, hire a contractor with knowledge of marketing and the effective use of radio and television, and let the soldiers be soldiers. Let them provide security for the experts in other fields.

In a recent symposium in *Harper's* ("Undoing Bush," June 2007), Edward Luttwak suggests using the military to destroy terrorist infrastructures, training camps, supply depots, etc., in raids that would not entail the nation building of the current campaigns. The State Department could issue warnings, brandishing reports from the CIA [Central Intelligence Agency], about the bad actors at work in the area; then the military raids would happen as a last resort, an instrument of foreign policy, not another movement by a permanent force embedded in the landscape and conducting what amounts to a unilateral foreign policy. Once a foreign government sees, through the exercise of military strength, how serious the U.S. intentions are, its own nation building can begin. Our military's only job would be to provide the baseline amount of security necessary for our advisers on the ground.

Other areas will require extensive reform as well. In the same symposium, James Bamford points out the need for intelligence services to be independent of the military. While the military will have to play a major role in intelligence gathering, the department calling the shots should be the CIA, not the Pentagon.

This would cut down on some of the turf wars that facilitated the intelligence failures leading up to 9/11 [2001 terrorist attacks], and make it harder for the Pentagon to sell a war without solid proof of the weapons that are the justification for intervention.

The military has many other MOSs (Military Occupational Specialties, or "jobs" in civilian parlance) that can be eliminated once it stops being a workfare program.

Great cuts can be made in health care, finance, and supply that would free the U.S. Army to become again what it had been since 1775, the greatest fighting organization in the history of the world.

| "An American-led campaign against the
 [Somali] pirates is warranted."

Multilateral Military Efforts Are Necessary to End Piracy

Michael B. Oren

Unlike the Barbary pirates who held American ships for ransom more than two hundred years ago, today's Somali pirates are targeting ships of all nations, ransoming cargo rather than sailors, maintains Michael B. Oren in the following viewpoint. He asserts that modern pirates pose a serious threat to international trade. Continuing to bargain with these pirates will only encourage further piracy, Oren notes. An American-led multilateral military campaign against the pirates, on the other hand, would deter today's pirates from escalating, he argues. Oren is a Georgetown University professor and the author of Power, Faith, and Fantasy: America in the Middle East, 1776 to the Present.

As you read, consider the following questions:

1. What are some of the prizes that the Somali pirates have seized, in Oren's view?

2. How does the author describe America's experience with the Barbary pirates?

3. In the author's opinion, what are some of the risks of an American-led campaign against the Somali pirates?

The attack began when an unidentified vessel drew alongside a merchant ship in the open sea and heavily armed brigands stormed aboard. "They made signs for us all to go forward," one of the frightened crewmen remembered, "assuring us in several languages that if we did not obey their commands they would massacre us all." The sailors were then stripped of all valuables and most of their clothing and locked in the hull of their own captured ship. They would be held in unspeakable conditions, subsisting on eight ounces of bread a day and threatened with beating and even beheading should they resist. "Death would be a great relief and more welcome than the continuance of our present situation," one of the prisoners lamented.

The Barbary Pirates Versus Today's Somali Pirates

The attack on the merchant ship, an American brig, occurred over 200 years ago in the Mediterranean during the scourge of the Barbary pirates. Sponsored by Morocco and the city-states of Tunis, Algiers, and Tripoli, the pirates preyed on civilian vessels, plundering their cargoes and kidnapping their crews. "It was written in the Koran . . . that it was their [the pirates'] right and duty to make war upon whoever they could find and to make slaves of all they could take as prisoners," the emissary of Tripoli's pasha [a high-ranking official of the Ottoman Empire] told a startled John Adams and Thomas Jefferson in London in 1785. The emissary demanded $1 million from the United States—one-tenth of the national budget—to suspend the assaults or face losing the valuable Mediterranean trade, representing one-fifth of all American exports.

The choice was excruciating. No longer protected by the British navy and lacking any gunboats of its own, the U.S. had no ready military option. Nor did it have international support. Jefferson's attempt to create an international coalition together with European states was summarily rejected. Defenseless and internationally isolated, most Americans were opposed to devoting their scarce resources to building a navy and instead favored following the age-old European custom of bribing the pirates—the euphemism was "tribute"—in exchange for safe passage. "Would to Heaven we had a navy to reform these enemies to mankind or crush them into nonexistence," an exasperated George Washington confided to his old comrade-in-arms, the Marquis de Lafayette.

Washington's frustration could well be echoed today in the face of escalating assaults by pirates from Somalia. Over 90 such attacks have occurred this year [in 2008] alone—a threefold increase since 2007—resulting in the capture of 14 ships and 250 of their crew members. Among their prizes, the pirates have seized a Ukrainian freighter crammed with Soviet-made battle tanks and, most recently, the tanker *Sirius Star* with $100 million worth of Saudi crude in its holds. These shipments are now being held off the Somali coast where the pirates are bargaining for their return.

Superficially, at least, there are many differences between the Somali pirates and their Barbary predecessors. The Somali bandits have no declared state sponsors and no avowed religious pretext. Their targets are no longer principally American ships but flags of all nations, including those of Arab states. And they are more interested in ransoming cargoes of arms and oil than hapless sailors. Yet, no less than in the 18th century, 21st-century piracy threatens international trade and confronts the U.S. with complex questions.

Confronting Complex Questions

Should the U.S. Navy, for example, actively combat the pirates, emulating the Indian warship that destroyed a Somali speedboat? Can the U.S., which is already overstretched militarily in two conflicts, afford to assume [in November 2008] responsibility for another open-ended operation in the same area? Or should America follow the example now being set by Saudi Arabia and various Asian states which, according to United Nations statistics, have paid $25 million to $30 million in ransoms to the pirates this year alone?

The answers to these questions can be gleaned from America's experience with Barbary. Lacking a navy and unwilling to bear the financial burden of building one, early American leaders opted to pay tribute to the pirates. By the 1790s, the U.S. was depositing an astonishing 20% of its federal income into North African coffers—this in addition to costly naval stores and even cannons and gunpowder. In return for this tribute, America only received more piracy. Foreign corporations refused to ship their goods in American hulls and U.S. diplomats were forced to sail overseas on

European-flagged ships for fear of seizure. Dozens of American sailors languished in captivity.

Demanding Action

Humiliated by these depredations, the American public grew critical of its feckless government and began to demand action. "Steer the hostile prow to Barb'ry's shores," wrote an anonymous poet, a veteran of the Battle of Bunker Hill, "release thy sons, and humble Africa's power." In response, in 1794, Congress passed a bill authorizing $688,888.82 for the construction of six frigates "adequate for the protection of the commerce of the U.S. against Algerian corsairs." By 1801, America possessed a navy capable of striking back at the pirates and a president willing to do so. In reply to Tripoli's declaration of war against the U.S., Thomas Jefferson ordered those frigates into battle.

Many setbacks would be suffered by U.S. naval forces in what was later called the Barbary Wars, not the least of which was the capture of the USS *Philadelphia* and its 307-man crew by Tripoli. Nevertheless, an intrepid trek by U.S. Marines and a mercenary force 500 miles across the Libyan desert—*to the shores of Tripoli*—in 1805 compelled the pirates to yield. Ten years later, President James Madison dispatched a fleet under Commodore Stephen Decatur to vanquish the remaining Barbary States. Shamed by these initiatives, the Europeans followed suit and sent their own warships to subdue the pirates, but the U.S. remained vigilant. A U.S. Mediterranean squadron—the forebear of today's Sixth Fleet—was kept on permanent patrol to ensure that Middle Eastern pirates never again threatened American commerce.

Of course, the world is a vastly more complicated place than it was two centuries ago and America's role in it, once peripheral, is now preeminent. Still, in the post-9/11 [2001 terrorist attacks] period, America would be ill-advised to act unilaterally against the pirates. The good news is: It does not have to. In contrast to the refusal to unite with America during the Barbary Wars, or more recently the Iraq War, the European states today share America's interest in restoring peace to the seas. Moreover, they have expressed a willingness to cooperate with American military measures against the Somali bandits. Unlike Washington and Jefferson, George W. Bush and Barack Obama need not stand alone.

Such a campaign will not be risk-free. The danger exists that America and its allies will become bogged down indefinitely in seeking to locate and destroy an elusive foe. The operations may also prove costly at a time when America can least afford them. Finally, there is the constant headache of maintaining an international coalition which may contain members who, like many early Americans, prefer to bribe the pirates rather than fight them.

Leading the Campaign

In spite of the potential pitfalls, an America-led campaign against the pirates is warranted. Though the Somali pirates do not yet endanger American trade, they will be emboldened by a lack of forceful response. Any attempt to bargain with them and to pay the modern equivalent of tribute will beget more piracy. Now, as then, the only effective response to piracy is a coercive one. "We shall offer them liberal and enlightened terms," declared Commodore Decatur, "dictated at the mouths of our cannons." Or, as William Eaton, commander of the [U.S.] Marines' march to Tripoli, more poignantly put it: "There is but one language that can be held to these people, and this is terror."

The U.S. is no longer the fragile and isolated country it was in the 1780s. It today possesses unrivaled naval power that it projects globally and enjoys far-reaching international support for unleashing that power against pirates. And while it is true that U.S. forces are deeply committed elsewhere in the region, addressing the threat of Somali pirates must be made a national priority while there is still time. Much like terrorism, piracy, unless uprooted, will mushroom.

George Washington wished that America had a navy capable of crushing the "enemies to mankind"—that is, not only the enemies of the U.S. His vision is now a reality. We have only to recognize it.

> *"Using the Navy to combat piracy would put a 'large dent' in its operational capacity and detract from counterterrorism operations and wars in Iraq and Afghanistan."*

Military Efforts to Contain Piracy Are Unnecessary

David Herbert

The best solution to the problem of Somali pirates may be to do nothing, argues David Herbert in the following viewpoint. A multinational naval force has failed to stop piracy in the Gulf of Aden, and the pirates pose little threat to American ships, he claims. Since most attacks have been relatively nonviolent, in the eyes of many companies the cost and liability of hiring private security forces is too high, Herbert contends. Moreover, while a U.S. military presence might deter some attacks, it would divert much-needed resources from counterterrorist efforts, he concludes. Herbert is a staff writer for the National Journal.

As you read, consider the following questions:

1. According to Herbert, what is piracy about at its core?

2. What does the author contend would be the cost of hiring armed guards to protect a ship?

3. In the author's opinion, what do insurance companies encourage shipowners to do when faced with piracy?

At three hearings since April 30, senators have interrogated a raft of mariners, shipowners, Defense and State department officials, and policy wonks about ways to combat Somali piracy. Arm the crews? Hire armed guards? Send in the Marines? Sen. Tom Udall, D-N.M., boiled down the confusion and frustration: "What is the solution here?" he asked. "How do we get our ships protected?"

No one was ready to supply the real answer: We don't.

Very simply, last month's dramatic rescue of Capt. Richard Phillips, in which Navy snipers took out his pirate captors, has given us an inflated view of what we can do to stop Somali pirates. Despite a multinational naval force, attacks off the Gulf of Aden and eastern coast of Somalia increased tenfold in the first quarter of 2009 over the same period last year. At its core, piracy is about economics, and neither private industry nor the world's governments are prepared to spend the necessary money or political capital to end the threat. Considering the minimal risk to U.S.-flagged ships and a host of potential silver linings in this brigandry, that just might be OK.

If you want to understand why pirates will continue to operate with impunity off the Somali coast, follow the money.

A growing consensus among military and industry figures says that putting security teams aboard ships can repel and deter pirate attacks—the successful defense of the Italian cruise liner MSC *Melody* last month by private Israeli guards reinforced that view. The trouble is finding someone to pay for them.

The shipping industry, hit hard by the economic downturn and already operating on razor-thin profit margins, can't afford to defend itself. Since May 2008, London-based maritime insurers have slapped shipowners with $20,000-a-trip (or more) premiums for sailing through pirate-infested waters off Somalia. But it's still cheaper for owners to pay those premiums and chip in for the occasional ransom than to hire armed guards, which industry sources and the Congressional Research Service estimate would cost $40,000 to $60,000 per transit.

Hiring private security guards also presents potential legal liabilities. Witness Blackwater in Iraq. "You would end up with some cowboys . . . shooting some poor fisherman," said Per Gullestrup, CEO of Copenhagen-based Clipper Projects, who negotiated the release of his ship CEC *Future* and its 13 crew members after pirates captured it last fall. "That becomes the owner's problem."

Lawmakers are pushing shipowners to arm their crews, which might be a cheaper option. But even if legal issues could be resolved (many ports don't want weapons brought into harbor), the potential for an accidental death (and expensive lawsuit) and higher insurance rates have scared off most companies.

The relative nonviolence of the Somali attacks—four mariners died in pirates' hands out of 815 hostages taken in 2008—has made living with piracy even more palatable to shipowners, explained Peter Leeson, author of *The Invisible Hook: The Hidden Economics of Pirates*. "The idea of arming crews or hiring guards has failed the market test," said Leeson, an economics professor at George Mason University. "The fact that [shipowners] are not doing it means it's not the cheapest thing to do."

If shippers had their way, navies from around the world would be footing the bill for security, either by stationing marines on ships or sending more warships to patrol and shepherd convoys. But the U.S. Defense Department and lawmakers have balked.

There is "no doubt" that an increased military presence would help disrupt and deter attacks, Navy Vice Adm. James A. Winnefeld testified at a Senate Armed Services Committee hearing last week. But using the Navy to combat piracy would put a "large dent" in its operational capacity and detract from counterterrorism operations and wars in Iraq and Afghanistan, to say nothing of the tremendous cost of these operations.

Pirates aren't the only ones profiting from this deadlock: Maritime insurance companies are raking in hundreds of millions of dollars from piracy premiums, explained J. Peter Pham, the director of the Nelson Institute for International and Public Affairs at James Madison University. Back-of-the-envelope calculations reveal just how much: 20,000 ships sailing through these waters every year paying $20,000 or more each in premiums adds up to at least $400 million a year. Insurers, who largely oppose arming crews or putting security teams aboard ships, have paid out $100 million in ransoms at most, Pham estimated. "As far as the London-based insurers are concerned, business as usual is good business," he said. "They are not going to be the group lobbying for a crackdown on piracy."

Insurance companies typically encourage owners to pay ransoms rather than forcibly take back ships (which could put an insurer on the line for damage to a ship worth far more money than any ransom). Gullestrup's insurer persuaded him to let it pay a ransom between $1 million and $2 million to recover his hijacked ship (he won't release the exact figure, to avoid jeopardizing negotiations for other owners). Meanwhile, ransom payments are edging higher.

Senators talked tough at a string of recent hearings, repeatedly citing the line in the Marine Corps hymn about "the shores of Tripoli"—a reference to the First Barbary War—as a historical precedent for military action. That war, however, was fought against the sultanate of Tripoli and resulted in an

The Dangers of Deadly Force

Some shipping experts worry that using deadly force in hopes of deterring the pirates could backfire. "We are already concerned that last week's [in April 2009] rescue operation could increase the level of violence," says Hannah Koep, . . . [an analyst who] advises insurers and shipowners on piracy-related issues. In lawless and impoverished Somalia, adds [journalist] Jim Wilson, . . . "life is cheap. If you kill one pirate, someone is going to take his place. If you kill a hundred pirates, hundreds will take their place. . . . If you are going to go around shooting people, you are going to radicalize the [Somali] population."

Mark Hosenball and Michael Isikoff,
"Blood in the Water," Newsweek, April 15, 2009.

official peace treaty. It was not at all like today's piracy by criminal syndicates in a failed state.

The seafaring nations don't have much of a plan for prosecuting brigands. The U.S. and Europe, worried that creative legal defenses and prosecutors' unfamiliarity with maritime law might result in not-guilty verdicts or short prison terms, have been generally reluctant to try pirates at home; acquitted pirates would also have strong cases to ask for asylum. The U.S., the European Union, and the United Kingdom have inked agreements with Kenya to prosecute pirates locally, but the Kenyan courts lack the capacity (and sometimes the will) to prosecute hundreds of cases.

Conventional wisdom holds that the only long-term solution is shoring up the transitional government in Somalia and helping it develop a coast guard. That may not be possible in the short term, however. Leeson questioned whether the kind of tenuous stability the transitional government is offering is the answer. The town of Eyl in the Somali province of Puntland has something closer to a genuine government, he pointed out, but is also the base for many pirate attacks in the Gulf of Aden.

Equipping Somalis to patrol the coast could just as easily turn into a training program for future pirates, argued a report released last week by Enough, the anti-genocide project of the Center for American Progress. "There is a well-established tradition of shifting militia membership in Somalia," said John Prendergast, a Clinton White House Africa adviser who co-wrote the report. "Our view is that with a little training and a small, subsidized salary, that training would be quickly targeted by pirate recruiters."

So what should Washington do? Maybe nothing.

American-flagged ships make up just a fraction of the maritime traffic in the Gulf of Aden. As few as one out of the 70 to 80 ships in the Gulf of Aden on any given day flies the Stars and Stripes, and only two American-flagged ships have been attacked—Capt. Phillips's MV *Maersk Alabama* and, a few days after Phillips was freed, the MV *Liberty Sun*, which outran its attackers.

Piracy may even have a silver lining. The marauding is already drawing attention to the humanitarian crisis and political unrest onshore, which the U.S. has largely steered clear of since pulling out of Somalia in the early 1990s after 19 American soldiers were killed there. In recent years, U.S. interest in Somalia has been largely related to terrorism. The pirate attacks began spiking after the U.S.-backed invasion of Somalia by Ethiopia in 2006, which was intended to unseat an Islamist government.

Prendergast and Enough hope that piracy will help drive a more nuanced American policy toward Somalia. "There has to be action on both levels," he said. "We've seen a huge response in respect to naval armadas being sent to the Gulf of Aden and the Red Sea, but we have not seen a remotely correspond-ing investment in state reconstruction."

In the immediate term, piracy is giving new urgency to U.S. adoption of the United Nations Convention on the Law of the Sea, which clarifies international maritime laws and for-malizes rules for interdicting pirates. The agreement has bi-partisan support in Congress and the backing of the military, environmentalists, deep-sea drillers, and just about everyone else, but it has languished in committee for years, partly be-cause of inattention and partly because of stiff opposition from some conservative senators.

The other good news is that piracy doesn't last forever. The heyday of marauding in the 18th-century Caribbean, im-mortalized today in Disney rides and Hollywood blockbusters, lasted only a decade, Leeson explained, before the toll on ship-ping forced the British navy to clear out pirate enclaves. Until today's shipping industry and governments reach that eco-nomic tipping point: ahoy.

> *"The Defense Department is the only department in government that has the personnel, equipment, and command and control capabilities to rapidly respond to disasters within the United States."*

Armed Forces Play an Important Role in Disaster Relief

Derek Reveron

The resources available to the U.S. Department of Defense (DoD) make the armed forces well equipped to respond quickly to national disasters, maintains Derek Reveron in the following viewpoint. The DoD has more personnel, equipment, and command capabilities than most state agencies, he argues. Indeed, Reveron reasons, the success of the military's contribution to the Hurricane Katrina relief effort demonstrates its effectiveness. Fears that the military would abuse this role are unwarranted and do not reflect public opinion, he asserts. Reveron, professor of national security affairs at the Naval War College, is a former intelligence analyst for the FBI.

As you read, consider the following questions:

1. In Reveron's opinion, what has been the effect of the Posse Comitatus Act?

2. According to the author, why isn't there any reason to think the military would lose its warfighting edge if it engaged in domestic relief operations?

3. In the author's view, what will happen if the Department of Homeland Security cannot overcome its bureaucratic shortfalls and leadership deficiencies?

Hurricane Katrina exposed the country's weaknesses in disaster preparation and disaster relief. Americans affected by the storm and those watching it on TV expected a quick, competent response to rescue those stranded, feed those hungry, and secure those vulnerable to the chaos that ensued. While the congressional hearings are just beginning and blame is volleyed among local, state, and federal officials, one thing is clear: The Defense Department's Joint Task Force [Katrina] commander, Lieutenant General Russel Honoré, will survive the inquiry as a hero, because Defense was so integral and successful throughout the relief effort.

The military's success has sparked anew the debate on the proper role of the military in a democratic society. Though traditional boundaries between the military and civilian authorities have been blurring over the decades, Katrina raises an important civil-military relations question: What should be the military's role in disaster relief and other non-warfighting activities in the United States?

Nature Can Be a Devastating Enemy

Recently, President [George W.] Bush urged Congress to consider this question and whether the Defense Department should play a primary role in disaster relief. Currently, the military is only the lead to dissuade, deter, and defeat enemy attacks upon the U.S., the population, and critical infrastructure. As the *Strategy for Homeland Defense and Civil Support* makes clear, the Department of Defense only provides support to civil authorities in other circumstances. But as hurricanes Katrina and Rita made clear, nature can be a devastating enemy. If we focus on the result and not the cause of the devastation, then the Defense Department should play more than a supporting role in disaster relief. To the disappointment of many in defense circles, no other federal or state agency is as well resourced and as competent as the Defense Department.

Initial response to the president's call for an increased role of the military as America's 911 [emergency] force object on the grounds of Posse Comitatus. In 1878, Congress passed the Posse Comitatus Act to prohibit the use of the military in a law enforcement role. While few civilians grasp or care about the historical reasons for enacting Posse Comitatus or the legal distinctions between active-duty military (Title 10) and the National Guard (Title 32), the effect of the act was to remove America's most capable force from a direct role in operating within the United States.

The Defense Department is the only department in government that has the personnel, equipment, and command and control capabilities to rapidly respond to disasters within the United States. The current challenge facing the country is when to employ the military. The approach outlined in the National Response Plan and current history suggest there are not unambiguous answers.

Expanding the Use of the Military

Since it is an act of Congress, it can be changed. In fact, Congress and the president have consistently expanded the use of the military in domestic affairs because the security and disaster relief challenges can frequently exceed the ability of local governments and other federal agencies to respond. For decades, for example, the military has assisted law enforcement

A Limited, but Important Role

In a major disaster, the military can play an important role by bringing to bear equipment, trainings, and expertise vital to rapid and efficient relief efforts. But these skills are not law enforcement. They include providing shelter, clearing debris, providing rescue operations and other physical operations requiring sophisticated logistical coordination and execution. . . . The military cannot, and should not, be asked to function as a domestic law enforcement entity. The Department of Defense (DoD) is amongst the most vocal supporters of this position. To begin with, DoD sees its mission as warfighting. Redirecting resources to domestic operations can serve to weaken the military's warfighting capability. Therefore, relief undertakings should be quick and limited to the immediate needs that the equipment and training of the military can fulfill.

Randall Jackson,
"Posse Comitatus and the Military's Role in Disaster Relief,"
Critical Infrastructure Protection Program, Core CIP Research,
February 2006. http://cip.gmu.edu.

to combat the illegal flow of drugs. More recently, the military has been preparing to respond to a nuclear, chemical, or biological event. The reasoning is simple: The task of preventing or cleaning up a mass casualty event is too great for local officials, so the real question is *when* should we employ the military. The approach outlined in the National Response Plan, as well as current history, suggests there are not unambiguous answers.

Since 9/11 [2001 terrorist attacks], there have been calls for expanding the role of the military in nontraditional spheres. My colleague Jeff Norwitz argues that the nature of counterterrorism requires that the Defense Department engage more on U.S. territory than it currently does. The Defense Department, however, has not been eager to employ forces on domestic soil. In fact, it wasn't until 2002 that Northern Command was created to plan, organize, and execute homeland defense and civil support missions. This new role has meant deploying surface-to-air missiles around the national capital, conducting combat air patrols over American cities, and developing an awareness of threats in the maritime approaches to the United States. We no longer think of terrorism as a problem to be addressed by law enforcement agencies alone. It's time we revised our thinking about natural disasters as well.

The Military Can Be Reliable in Domestic Operations

These images show the positive contributions the military made in the wake of the hurricanes: vaccinating Americans, repairing buildings, and providing clean water. These are the types of things the Defense Department has been doing for people all around the world for decades. American service members have built schools in the Balkans, so why shouldn't they do the same in the U.S.? The American military delivered food to tsunami victims in Indonesia, so why shouldn't it deliver food to hurricane victims in the Gulf Coast? And American soldiers and marines provide security in Iraq and Afghanistan, so why shouldn't they in times of crisis in New Orleans? Historical reasons and deference to local authorities are not sufficient answers.

There is no reason to think that that military would abuse an expanded role helping Americans or that an expanded role would run counter to American political culture. Public opinion polls consistently show that Americans trust the military to do what is right. A January 2005 Harris Poll shows that 63 percent trust the military compared to only 22 percent who trust Congress.

There is no reason to think that the military would lose its warfighting edge if it were engaged in domestic relief operations. The current defense structure relies on dual-capable forces for domestic consequence management and other non-combat activities. Multipurpose platforms like aircraft carriers or amphibious landing ships consistently prove their worth in flexibility. Responses after the Asian tsunami or hurricanes Katrina and Rita illustrate that the Navy can use its ships to stage search-and-rescue operations, to serve as floating hospitals, and to produce much-needed water for disaster-stricken areas (millions of gallons a day).

The Effectiveness of Military Leaders

Nor would the warfighting tradition be dulled while performing "soft missions" like disaster relief. As I explored in the book *America's Viceroys*, the military has been fulfilling an important role in diplomacy and non-warfighting missions for decades. For example, it was Gen. Anthony Zinni who maintained relations with countries in Central Asia long before Afghanistan became important to the United States. It was Gen. Charles Wilhelm who assisted Bogotá's efforts to stabilize Colombia. And it was Admiral William Crowe who created diplomatic opportunities throughout the Asia-Pacific region. These non-warfighting missions did not undermine their effectiveness as military officers.

There are many more examples of military leaders proving they could broadly represent the United States, negotiate difficult treaties, and meet the challenges civilian leaders designate. With the shortcomings of the D.C.-based bureaucracies and limitations of local governments to respond to major events, military leaders have a distinct advantage over their civilian counterparts: The military breeds success; the officer promotion system ensures that only the best rise to the top and once there these officers are endowed with large planning staffs, solid command and control capabilities, and an infrastructure to move personnel, equipment, and supplies.

And senior military officers continue their non-warfighting roles during "retirement." Admiral Crowe represented the United States in London; Admiral [Joseph W.] Prueher served in Beijing; General Zinni was President George W. Bush's special envoy to the Middle East. Consequently, the military has a reputation for getting things done and its "can do" attitude towards any crisis is what provoked the current discussion on disaster relief duties. Why shouldn't we see military leaders fill similar positions within domestic security? Lieutenant General Honoré is perfectly qualified to be the secretary of Homeland Security. Vice Admiral [Thad] Allen could no doubt lead an enlarged FEMA [Federal Emergency Management Agency] that has disaster preparation, mitigation, and response capabilities. The long-term question is whether civilian agencies can develop competence and strong leadership equal to that of the military. If the Department of Homeland Security cannot overcome its bureaucratic shortfalls and leadership deficiencies, then the Defense Department will be looked at to perform more and more domestic noncombat missions.

The military is a proven contributor to foreign policy. Why can't it make the same contributions to domestic policy? In a time of crisis, the United States doesn't need a coordinator; it needs a leader. Civilian-controlled military officers offer this leadership. Why shouldn't the Defense Department be the lead organization for domestic disasters?

| "The creation of an active-duty military force ... that could be used to suppress public protest here at home is a very bad sign."

Training Armed Forces to Quell Domestic Unrest Is Troubling

Amy Goodman

Training a military combat brigade to respond to civil unrest in the United States is a frightening sign, argues Amy Goodman in the following viewpoint. Claims that weapons would not be used unless approved at the highest level are not reassuring when at the 2008 Republican National Convention, National Guard troops were dispatched to discourage protest, she maintains. At times of vast economic disparity and a costly, unpopular war, creation of a force to suppress public protest is discouraging to those who value freedom, she reasons. Goodman is a syndicated columnist and host of Democracy Now! *an international TV/ radio news hour.*

As you read, consider the following questions:

1. In Goodman's view, why is talk of trouble on U.S. streets omnipresent?

2. To what does the author claim is akin to arresting almost fifty journalists at the Republican National Convention?

3. What example does the author provide to illustrate the risk of a massive crackdown on dissent?

A little-noticed story surfaced a couple of weeks ago [in September 2008] in the *Army Times* newspaper about the 3rd Infantry Division's 1st Brigade Combat Team [BCT]. "Beginning Oct. 1 for 12 months," reported *Army Times* staff writer Gina Cavallaro, "the 1st BCT will be under the day-to-day control of U.S. Army North, the Army service component of Northern Command, as an on-call federal response force for natural or manmade emergencies and disasters, including terrorist attacks." Disturbingly, she writes that "they may be called upon to help with civil unrest and crowd control" as well.

An Armed Domestic Force

The force will be called the chemical, biological, radiological, nuclear or high-yield explosive Consequence Management Response Force. Its acronym, CCMRF, is pronounced "sea-smurf." These "sea-smurfs," Cavallaro reports, have "spent 35 of the last 60 months in Iraq patrolling in full battle rattle," in a combat zone, and now will spend their 20-month "dwell time"—time troops are required to spend to "reset and regenerate after a deployment"—armed and ready to hit the U.S. streets.

The *Army Times* piece includes a correction stating that the forces would not use nonlethal weaponry domestically. I called Air Force Lieutenant Colonel Jamie Goodpaster, a pub-

Avoiding Unintended Consequences

There is no doubt that when things go really badly—in terms of a disaster or civil disturbance—the military possesses unique equipment and training capabilities that can lend stability to a fractious situation. But when they created a republic in which the rule of law and civilian control of the military are founding principles, the Founding Fathers placed tight legal constraints on the standing army's ability to take to the streets and expected such use to end at the earliest possible juncture to restore the status quo.

While the military is one of the most admired institutions in the country today, operational planners recognize that unintended consequences can occur when veteran combat soldiers are placed in a position of authority over anxious civilians in a chaotic environment. Tired, stressed teenagers with weapons make mistakes, and when those mistakes are made on the national stage during a domestic upheaval, the consequences will be severe both personally and politically.

Craig Trebilcock,
"Resurrecting Posse Comitatus in the Post-9/11 World,"
Army Magazine, *May 2009.*

lic affairs officer for Northern Command. She told me that the overall mission was humanitarian, to save lives and help communities recover from catastrophic events. Nevertheless, the military forces would have weapons on-site, "containerized," she said—that is, stored in containers—including both lethal and so-called nonlethal weapons. They would have mostly wheeled vehicles, but would also, she said, have access to tanks. She said that use of weapons would be made at a higher level, perhaps at the secretary of defense level.

Talk of trouble on U.S. streets is omnipresent now, with the juxtaposition of Wall Street and Main Street. The financial crisis we face remains obscure to most people; titans of business and government officials assure us that the financial system is "on the brink," that a massive bailout is necessary, immediately, to prevent a disaster. Conservative and progressive members of Congress, at the insistence of constituents, blocked the initial plan. If the economy does collapse, if people can't go down to the bank to withdraw their savings, or get cash from an ATM, there may be serious "civil unrest," and the "sea-smurfs" may be called upon sooner than we imagine to assist with "crowd control."

The political and financial establishments seem completely galled that people would actually oppose their massive bailout, which rewards financiers for gambling. Normal people worry about paying their bills, buying groceries and gas, and paying rent or a mortgage in increasingly uncertain times. No one ever offers to bail them out. Wall Street's house of cards has collapsed, and the rich bankers are getting little sympathy from working people.

That's where the sea-smurfs come in. Officially formed to respond to major disasters, like a nuclear or biological attack, this combat brigade falls under the U.S. Northern Command, a military structure formed on October 1, 2002, to "provide command and control of Department of Defense homeland defense efforts." Military participation in domestic operations was originally outlawed with the Posse Comitatus Act in 1878. The John Warner National Defense Authorization Act for Fiscal Year 2007, however, included a section that allowed the president to deploy the armed forces to "restore public order" or to suppress "any insurrection." While a later bill repealed this, President [George W.] Bush attached a signing statement that he did not feel bound by the repeal.

A Crackdown on Dissent

We are in a time of increasing economic disparity, with the largest gap between rich and poor of any wealthy industrialized country. We are witnessing a crackdown on dissent, most recently with $100 million spent on "security" at the Democratic and Republican national conventions. The massive paramilitary police forces deployed at the RNC [Republican National Convention] in St. Paul, Minnesota, were complete overkill, discouraging protests and conducting mass arrests (National Guard troops just back from Fallujah were there). The arrest there of almost 50 journalists (myself included) showed a clear escalation in attempting to control the message (akin to the ban on photos of flag-draped coffins of dead soldiers). There are two ongoing, unpopular wars that are costing lives and hundreds of billions of dollars. Nobel-winning economist Joe Stiglitz estimates that Iraq alone will cost more than $3 trillion.

In December 2001, in the midst of restricted access to bank accounts due to a financial crisis, respectable, middle-class Argentineans rose up, took to the streets, smashed bank windows and ultimately forced the government out of power, despite a massive police crackdown and a failed attempt to control the media. Here in the U.S., with the prospect of a complete failure of our financial system, the people have spoken and do not want an unprecedented act of corporate welfare. We don't know how close the system is to collapse, nor do we know how close the people are to taking to the streets. The creation of an active-duty military force, the sea-smurfs, that could be used to suppress public protest here at home is a very bad sign.

Periodical Bibliography

The following articles have been selected to supplement the diverse views presented in this chapter.

Seth Cropsey
"To the Shores of Tripoli . . . The Place to Stop Pirates Is on the Beaches," *Weekly Standard*, vol. 14, no. 12, December 8, 2008.

William Norman Grigg
"Toward a Militarist America: The Framers of Our Republic Warned of the Dangers Posed by Overgrown Military Establishments. Could Our Nation Someday Succumb to a Military Dictatorship?" *New American*, January 9, 2006.

Stefan Halper
"Avoiding Disaster in Afghanistan," *American Spectator*, March 2009.

Gene Healy
"Who Is Watching the Watchmen?" *Washington DC Examiner*, May 5, 2009.

Mary Kaldor
"New Thinking in the Pentagon," *Peace Magazine*, January–March 2009.

Richard H. Kohn
"Coming Soon: A Crisis in Civil-Military Relations," *World Affairs*, Winter 2008.

Michael G. Mullen
"Military Must Stay Apolitical," *Joint Forces Quarterly*, July 2008.

Mackubin Thomas Owens
"Soldiers Aren't Cops," *National Review*, August 1, 2002.

Kelley Beaucar Vlahos
"Homeland Offense: Washington Contemplates Deploying the Armed Forces for Domestic Law Enforcement," *American Conservative*, February 9, 2009.

Bryan D. Watson
"A Look Down the Slippery Slope: Domestic Operations, Outsourcing, and the Erosion of Military Culture," *Air & Space Power Journal*, Spring 2008.

Who Should Serve in the Armed Forces?

Chapter Preface

Finding young men and women willing to serve in the U.S. armed forces has become increasingly difficult, particularly since the wars in Iraq and Afghanistan have grown increasingly unpopular. Adding to the challenges faced by military recruiters is the growing need for fresh recruits. The war on terror has stretched U.S. troops thin. Today's recruiters are, in fact, facing the toughest conditions ever faced by the nation's all-volunteer army. To meet their goals, desperate recruiters are contacting high school students and doing so with the benefit of Section 9528 of the No Child Left Behind (NCLB) Act of 2001, which gives military recruiters the same access to secondary school students as recruiters from postsecondary institutions or prospective employers. Not all approve of this policy, particularly concerned parents. In fact, many parent groups actively counter these efforts through campaigns to keep recruiters away from their high school children. Indeed, one of several controversies in the debate over who should serve in the armed forces is whether U.S. military recruiters should be granted access to high school campuses.

Opponents of the law argue that high schools should be safe places that are conducive to learning. These critics claim that recruiting quota pressures have forced recruiters to bend the rules, making their presence on campus dangerous and threatening. Indeed, several high-profile cases support this claim. In May 2005, an NBC affiliate in Cincinnati, Ohio, filmed military recruiters making false statements to high school students about the relative safety of Iraq compared to the United States. In fact, critics assert, some recruiters completely ignore the war in Iraq when talking to potential recruits. Opponents also fear the emphasis placed on the money enlistees will earn rather than on the dangers they face in combat. Critics point to the fact that recruiters often target lower-income students. Representative Charles B. Rangel of New York called current recruitment efforts an "economic draft" designed to lure the poor who cannot afford other career options.

Supporters disagree. In fact, they assert, for many lower-income students, military service may be the best opportunity available. Underprivileged recruits can, in fact, earn thousands of dollars in college aid to help them pursue a lucrative career. In an April 15, 2005, editorial, the *Seattle Times* asserts, "This country's all-volunteer army is indeed made up of mostly working-class men and women, including a higher percentage of minorities than in the general population. It has also done more to equalize opportunity and shift people into higher brackets of income than any industry." Proponents reason that military recruiters should therefore be granted the same access as job and college recruiters. Moreover, they argue, public schools, funded by the federal government, have a civic duty to support the military. Efforts to keep recruiters off campuses, they argue, also create a further divide between civilians and the military. The editors of the *St. Petersburg Times* on May 30, 2005, argue, "To ban military recruiters from the nation's high schools and colleges sends the wrong message to the men and women in uniform who risk their lives to serve their country."

The controversy over military recruiting at high schools remains heated as recruiters struggle to meet their quotas. The authors in the following chapter explore other controversies in the debate surrounding who should serve in the armed forces.

| "The solution is obvious: We must reinstate the draft."

The United States Should Reinstate the Draft

Bill Maxwell

The United States should bring back the draft to improve the quality of recruits, claims Bill Maxwell in the following viewpoint. To meet recruitment goals, the Department of Defense has reduced both the percentage of recruits required to have high school diplomas and the minimum score required on aptitude tests, he asserts. The costs of enlistment bonuses have also risen significantly, Maxwell maintains. The solution to lower standards and rising costs is to return to the draft and make military service mandatory, he concludes. Maxwell is a journalist with Florida's St. Petersburg Times.

As you read, consider the following questions:

1. What inspired Maxwell to return to the subject of bringing back the draft?

Bill Maxwell, "Time to Bring Back the Military Draft," *St. Petersburg Times*, vol. 31, November 5, 2006, p. 3P. Copyright © 2006 St. Petersburg Times. Reproduced by permission.

2. What does the author claim is distracting Americans from the demoralization of our all-volunteer fighting force?

3. In the opinion of Nicholas Confessore, what should be a condition of admission to college?

A column of mine on this same topic, the military draft, was published in the *St. Petersburg Times* on September 29, 1999. The headline was "Military service should be mandatory."

Again, we should bring back the draft.

Demoralization in the Armed Forces

I was inspired to return to this subject because of the furor [2004 presidential candidate] John Kerry created the other day when, while addressing students in Los Angeles, he lamely joked about George W. Bush's incuriosity and intellectual deficits, saying, "Education, if you make the most of it, you study hard, you do your homework and you make an effort to be smart, you can do well. If you don't, you get stuck in Iraq."

Instead of using Kerry's gaffe as a springboard to an honest national discussion about Bush's wrecking of our military, too many of us are letting the GOP's [Grand Old Party's, i.e. the Republican Party's] putrefaction machine distract us from the reality on the ground in Iraq and the demoralization of our all-volunteer fighting force.

The U.S. armed services, even the Army, the biggest supplier of troops to Iraq and Afghanistan, met their 2006 wartime recruiting goals. But the price has been high, and it may do permanent, irreparable harm to the enlisted ranks.

Following are some of the major concessions the services were forced to make. (My source is the Military Officers Association of America.)

Recruit quality has been affected. Until now, the Defense Department wanted 90 percent of boots [recruits] to have a high school diploma, and 60 percent to score above the median on armed forces aptitude tests. [In 2006], only 82 percent of Army recruits had diplomas, and 61 percent met the aptitude test standards—down from 92 percent and 72 percent, respectively, since 2004.

Enlistment standards have been changed. The Army, for example, increased its maximum enlistment age first from 35 to 40 last January, then to 42 in June. Most recently, the Army loosened restrictions on tattoos, criminal infractions, and a host of other old red flags.

Bonus budgets have skyrocketed. Enlistment bonus costs jumped from $166 million in 2005 to $238 million in 2006. Reenlistment bonus costs for fiscal year 2006 went past $650 million, versus an average of $120 million for fiscal years 2000–2004. If reenlistments drop, as they are expected to, recruiting goals will rise exponentially.

"The recruiting problem is not just an Army problem," General Richard Cody, the Army's vice chief of staff, told NBC News. "This is America's problem. And what we have to really do is talk about service to the nation—and a sense of duty to this nation."

Recruiting in the regular ranks is being hurt by many problems, such as longer and more frequent tours in Iraq, erratic schedules and the rising lethality of the fighting. Reservists also face these problems, with the added pressures of discontent at their daytime jobs, financial ruin and longer-than-expected deployments.

Seeking Solutions

Pentagon officials are desperately seeking solutions to this manpower crisis. While they are tinkering with shorter enlistment terms and talking of using current troops more efficiently, the big, bad gorilla remains in the middle of the floor: We need many more troops.

According to most analyses, recruitment is being hurt mostly by the appeal of college. That is right. More and more high school graduates are attending college without giving the military a second thought. Officials are trying to find attractive ways to lure college graduates into volunteering during this time of war. Based on everything I read, no gimmick or battery of gimmicks will work.

The solution is obvious: We must reinstate the draft. As Gen. Cody said, we are talking about "service to the nation" and "a sense of duty to the nation." I believe that every able-bodied, mentally fit U.S. citizen has a duty to serve. I leave the logistics to the experts.

I agree with Nicholas Confessore, editor of *Washington Monthly*, in his March 2003 article for the magazine:

> Every year, a million young adults begin attending four-year colleges. As a condition of admission, those students could be required to serve their country for up to two years, in civilian national service programs like AmeriCorps, or homeland security efforts such as guarding nuclear plants, or . . . in the military. Some percentage would choose the latter, especially if they were to receive more GI [a member of the armed forces] Bill-type college aid as a reward for higher-risk duty.

Let us face a nasty truth about ourselves as U.S. citizens: When it comes to serving our great nation, we are AWOL [absent without leave]. This crisis, not a flubbed Kerry joke, should be our national discussion. We should be ashamed.

| "Maintaining freedom of occupational choice and relying on incentives to attract qualified individuals for our national defense is surely the most equitable method of procuring military manpower."

The United States Should Not Reinstate the Draft

Walter Y. Oi

Military service should be a matter of choice, asserts Walter Y. Oi in the following viewpoint. Claims that an all-volunteer force (AVF) is motivated only by money and benefits are flawed, he maintains. Serving the country, acquiring skills, and receiving specialized training are major motivators, Oi contends. Moreover, he argues, concerns that the AVF is not representative of the population are also unwarranted, as the AVF has a greater percentage of high school graduates than the general population. The most equitable way to staff military is by volunteers, he reasons. Oi, an economics professor at the University of Rochester, served on President Richard M. Nixon's Commission on an All-Volunteer Force.

Walter Y. Oi, "Should We Bring Back the Draft? Is the All-Volunteer Force a 'Mercenary Army?'" *Regulation*, vol. 30, Fall 2007, pp. 8–12. Copyright © 2007 by CATO Institute. Republished with permission of CATO, conveyed through Copyright Clearance Center, Inc.

As you read, consider the following questions:

1. In Oi's view, what well-known claim made by Uwe E. Reinhardt is untrue?

2. According to the author, why did Gen. Maxwell Thurman introduce a high-quality-personnel policy in the early 1980s?

3. In the author's opinion, what prediction concerning African Americans made by critics of ending the draft was not borne out?

For a quarter of a century, 1948–1973, young American men faced a military service obligation. They could be drafted to serve in the enlisted ranks for 24 months if the obligation was not discharged by deferment, exemption, or serving in the Reserves or active-duty forces as an enlisted man or officer. Conscription was abolished on July 1, 1973. Since that date, the basic training camps have been populated by young men and women who have voluntarily chosen the military over alternative civilian jobs and activities.

Stanford historian David M. Kennedy wrote in a 2006 *American Academy of Arts and Sciences Bulletin* article that this development is alarming: "The U.S. Armed Forces today have many of the attributes of a mercenary army." This essay asks if Kennedy's assessment is correct—is today's All-Volunteer Force (AVF) a mercenary army? Moreover, is the AVF representative of the population that it defends? Finally, how does the AVF depart from the composition of some hypothetical force that might emerge under some other method of manpower procurement? . . .

Stylized Facts and Fancies

Professor Kennedy is one of a number of writers on the AVF who assert a stylized fact: The young men and women who join today's armed services do so mainly for the money and benefits. From this stylized fact, critics of the AVF often jump to the assertion made by Princeton professor Uwe E. Reinhardt in a 2006 *Washington Post* op-ed: "It is well known that to fill the ranks, the Pentagon relies heavily on the bottom half of the nation's income distribution, sending recruiters to the slums and low-income neighborhoods." This may be "well known" but it is untrue; Reinhardt apparently has not looked at the data and instead is peddling a stylized fancy.

Let us consider the young people who serve in the AVF, and who served under the old conscription system. Obviously, under either system, not everyone is physically fit to serve. The Universal Military Training and Service Act, the draft law, judged mental fitness by an individual's score on the Armed Forces Qualification Test (AFQT). Those with a score of 10 or lower were placed in draft classification IV-F and exempted. When draft calls were low in relation to the pool of eligibles, the lower bound was raised. During the last decade under the draft, men with AFQT scores below 20 were deferred. A 1964 Army study reported that more than one-third of the nation was unfit—specifically, 35.6 percent of draft-eligible men who passed through armed forces examining stations failed to satisfy the physical and/or mental qualification standards.

Attritions are costly and were a problem even under the draft. In the first five years of the AVF, Congress allowed military pay to slip. To meet recruiting goals, the Army accepted lower-quality recruits, some with police records, even though military brass realized that there was a relation between quality and retention. In order to have 100 soldiers on board at the end of two years, the Army had to recruit, enlist, and train 131 high school graduates or 188 high school dropouts.

Higher-Quality Recruits

In the early 1980s, under the AVF, General Maxwell Thurman introduced a high-quality-personnel policy. Army recruiters were instructed to find young men who had a high school diploma and an AFQT score of 50 or higher, which means that recruits had to be from the top half of the mental test distribution. With higher-quality recruits, the Army was able to reduce the size of basic training camps by 27 percent. Additionally, brighter soldiers could handle the technical materials in the advanced individual training courses, which enabled the Army to upgrade its entry-level training. Thurman, in a chapter he contributed to the book *Professionals on the Front Line*, wrote:

> The existing Army training system was predicated on a World War II conscription supported mobilization scheme where training was just a phase in which all units participated before deployment. The Army had not adjusted to the point where training for combat was an integral part of daily peacetime activity for the AVF.

The structure of the AVF differs from that for a mixed conscript/volunteer force. The fraction of the force assigned to the combat arms (e.g., the infantry, armor, Airborne, Special Forces) is smaller under the AVF, with more service members in the supporting logistical tail. The Army has substituted capital and trained soldiers for raw, untrained labor. . . .

When enlisted Navy men were asked the reasons why they volunteered, "service to country" was a major response. Other responses included acquiring skills that will be useful in the civilian labor market, qualifying for post-service educational benefits, getting into the submarine corps or other special assignments, etc. Michael Hansen and Sam Kleinman reported in a 2005 Center for Naval Analyses study that "training to learn technical skills" was a major component of compensation in attracting youths to become sailors. Navy enlisted recruits do not behave like mercenaries. American sailors will postpone gratification to get training today, not at all like the carefree men in [20th-century Irish leader of battles in Africa and the Indian Ocean] Mike Hoare's mercenary army.

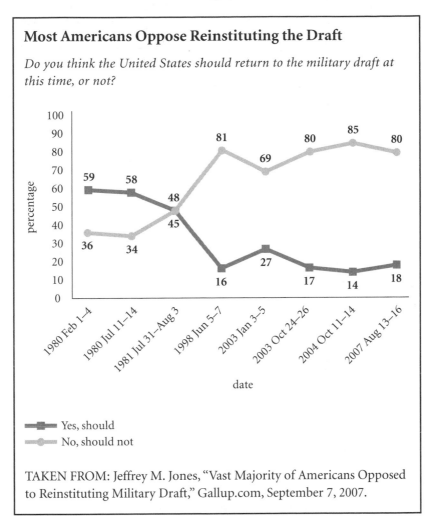

Most Americans Oppose Reinstituting the Draft

Do you think the United States should return to the military draft at this time, or not?

TAKEN FROM: Jeffrey M. Jones, "Vast Majority of Americans Opposed to Reinstituting Military Draft," Gallup.com, September 7, 2007.

The Characteristics of the AVF

The armed services have never been, and are not now, representative of the U.S. population. The characteristics of the active-duty forces depend on the method of manpower procurement, accession and retention policies, and the strength of the civilian labor market.

Conscription forced some men into involuntary service as enlisted men while others reluctantly volunteered so as to discharge their military service obligation. With the end of the draft, the armed services had to compete for individuals who were willing and able to satisfy the accession requirements.

The picture painted by Professor Kennedy is one in which the AVF had to enlist the least-productive individuals—the dregs of society. The facts reported by Russel Beland and Curtis Gilroy in a 2006 *Washington Post* op-ed contradict the Kennedy story of a mercenary army. I point out a few attributes of the force that have emerged when those who serve do so by choice, not coercion:

Gender. In 1973, the last year under conscription, women made up only 4 percent of the active-duty force. There was apparently little pressure to find, recruit, and train qualified women when men could be drafted. In the transition to the AVF, the share of women in uniform rose to 12 percent in 1990 and 15 percent in 2000. The role of women was also changing, as Aline Quester and Curtis Gilroy noted in a 2002 *Contemporary Economic Policy* paper.

Accession. Not everyone is fit to serve. In the last decade under the draft, 1964–73, a man was excused from military service (via exemption or deferment) if his score on the AFQT was under 20. The accession policy introduced by General Thurman in the early 1980s raised the minimum acceptable AFQT score to 30 as well as a high school diploma—a GED [General Educational Development] would not do.

Of course, the AFQT is not an accurate instrument. From January 1976 to October 1980, the Department of Defense slipped and mis-normed the test. Roughly 25 percent of Army accessions would not have met the mental qualification standard with a correctly normed test. The mistake has been corrected. Judged by mental test scores, the AVF in 2000 is considerably superior to its conscription-era counterpart.

Education. According to Kennedy, "While 46 percent of all Americans have some college education, only 6.5 percent of the 18- to 24-year-old enlisted men in the Army have ever seen the inside of a college classroom." But are AVF soldiers educationally inferior to the people they are defending? Beland and Gilroy, in their *Washington Post* op-ed, note that 90 percent of Army enlisted men have a high school diploma compared to 80 percent for the entire economy. Moreover, Kennedy ignores the AVF officers, nearly all of whom have graduated from college.

Income. Professor Reinhardt claimed that the vast majority of enlisted accessions are drawn from the bottom half of the income distribution. Yet, high-quality recruits with high school diplomas and strong mental test scores are unlikely to be found in slums and low-income census tracts. Beland and Gilroy found that the neighborhoods in which most Army enlistees resided had incomes above the average for all census tracts. They do not come from the bottom half of the income distribution.

Race. The armed services are equal employment opportunity employers. In 1995, only 7.6 percent of all college graduates were African American. However, 12.0 percent of all officers were African American. Blacks are overrepresented not only in the officer corps, but also in the enlisted ranks.

The presidential commissions on the draft chaired, respectively, by Burke Marshall in 1967–68 and Thomas S. Gates in 1969–70, heard witnesses who testified that African Americans were carrying more than their fair share of the defense burden in the Vietnam War. Some 30–40 percent of the soldiers in the infantry and combat arms were African Americans.

Critics of ending the draft predicted that a change to an AVF would result in those percentages rising and the nation would be protected with the blood of an all-black army. But that prediction was not borne out. In 1995, African American soldiers made up only 9 percent of the infantry in the AVF. Black volunteers chose military occupational specialties in supply, clerical, transport, and food services to enhance the chances of being promoted and retained. Contrary to the dire predictions, African American soldiers do not make up the majority of the soldiers on the front line. Instead, as noted in a 1999 *Wall Street Journal* headline, "Infantry Surprise: It's Now Mostly White; Blacks Hold Office Jobs." . . .

A Social Compact?

In his 2006 article, Professor Kennedy concluded that "a preponderant majority of Americans with no risk whatsoever of exposure to military service has in effect hired some of the least advantaged of their fellow countrymen to do some of their most dangerous business while they go on with their affairs unbloodied and undistracted." This is simply not so. The men and women who serve in today's AVF are not hired guns. Military pay was raised to be competitive with wages in the civilian labor market. It was the right thing to do, to eliminate the hidden tax that had been placed on draftees. Members of the AVF enlist to serve their country, to get training and postservice education benefits, and engage in something that is worth their while.

Professor Kennedy and draft proponent Representative Charles [B.] Rangel argue that in a democratic society, the burden of defense ought to be equitably shared. The composition of the AVF is not representative of the population it defends. But it must be remembered that the size of the Army in relation to the size of the U.S. population is smaller today than the armies that fought in Vietnam, Korea, or World War II. Kennedy and Rangel have proposed bringing back the draft, possibly embedded in a larger national service program in order to spread the defense burden. The very well-to-do and the highly educated have always been able to evade conscription. Maintaining freedom of occupational choice and relying on incentives to attract qualified individuals for our national defense is surely the most equitable method of procuring military manpower.

> "New technology, fresh attention to in-
> clusive leadership styles, and societal
> attitudes all favor a greater role for
> women."

The Role of Women in the Armed Forces Should Be Expanded

Holly Yeager

Women have been proving themselves in all branches of the armed forces, asserts Holly Yeager in the following viewpoint. In fact, while women are officially barred from serving in direct ground combat units, the blurred lines of combat in Iraq place women under fire and firing back, she claims. Despite critics' fears, women are not falling apart in the battlefield, nor have they had much impact on military readiness or morale, Yeager maintains. Nevertheless, she argues, barriers remain because changing military culture is difficult. Yeager is a Washington, D.C., journalist who writes about defense and women's issues.

Holly Yeager, "Soldiering Ahead," *Wilson Quarterly*, vol. 31, Summer 2007, pp. 54–62. Copyright © 2007 Woodrow Wilson International Center for Scholars, 2007. Reproduced by permission of the author.

As you read, consider the following questions:

1. According to Yeager, who had difficulty accepting Drill Sergeant Dymetra Bass when she moved to train artillery units?

2. Why, in the author's opinion, is the number of women's opportunities at the top of the command structure small today?

3. In the author's view, why does even the most outspoken critic of the Pentagon's gender policies not call for a rollback of women's roles in the military?

When Dymetra Bass was a drill sergeant, she had no trouble proving her mettle to the fresh Army recruits she pushed through basic training at Fort Leonard Wood in Missouri. "Every private would tell me, the meanest drill sergeants were the women drill sergeants," she says with a touch of pride. "We had to be so tough because people come from all walks of life. Some people, women have never told them what to do before."

Bass enlisted in 1989, right after high school, where she had been a cheerleader, and she arrived with an essential drill sergeant's tool: a booming voice. She also knew how to keep her soldiers motivated. "I like control, so it was easy for me. I like being in the front. I like leading. I believe in leading by example."

Proving Themselves

But things changed when Bass moved to Fort Sill, Oklahoma, in 1999 as part of the first group of female drill sergeants assigned to train new members of field artillery units—one of the few areas still closed to women. "It was the drill sergeants who couldn't accept us, because they were artillery, and then you bring these women in here to teach these civilians how to be soldiers, and teach them combat skills. . . . They didn't believe it could be done, or done the right way."

Bass had no background in artillery, but that didn't matter. Her job was to do basic training. But her male colleagues still worried that the women wouldn't be able to carry their load and that to pick up the slack, men would always have to run with the fastest group and demonstrate the most demanding drills, such as scurrying under barbed wire and using a rope to maneuver across water. "We had to prove ourselves a lot more," Bass says.

Female leaders up and down the U.S. military's chain of command—from noncommissioned officers such as Bass, who deal most directly with troops, to two- and three-star generals and admirals—talk about having to prove themselves, again and again. But slowly, and rather quietly, more and more women have been doing just that. Women make up 14.4 percent of enlisted personnel and 15.9 percent of the officer corps in the 1.4-million-strong active-duty U.S. military, according to the most recent Defense Department figures. That is a marked increase from the 1.6 percent of the military that was female in 1973, when the draft ended and new recruitment goals for women were set.

A Major Test

The war in Iraq has been a major test of women's new role in the military, and while a full assessment has yet to be completed—the RAND Corporation is at work on one—they seem to have performed well in the field. Women are now permitted to serve in more than 90 percent of military occupations, though they are still barred from jobs or units whose main mission is direct ground combat. But the fluid lines of conflict in Iraq have put the units in which women serve, such as military police, supply, and support, in the line of fire, challenging traditional ideas about what constitutes a "combat" position. "Women are fighting, they are in the struts and on the patrols," says Pat Foote, a retired Army brigadier general. "They are running the convoys, getting shot at and shooting back." The war's death toll reflects this battlefield reality: As of early June 2007, the nearly 3,500 U.S. service members who had lost their lives in Operation Iraqi Freedom included more than 70 women.

"Critics speculated a lot about what would happen if we let women in these jobs," notes Lory Manning, a retired Navy captain who directs the Women in the Military project at the Women's Research & Education Institute in Washington, D.C. "[They speculated that] the men couldn't do their jobs, that everyone would be pregnant, that they'd be so busy having sex that they couldn't do anything else."

"We now have units under fire with men and women in them," Manning says. "We have experience of women firing weapons. They don't fall to emotional bits."

Nor has the American public fallen to bits. The sometimes dramatic footage of women on the front lines, of women returning home to military hospitals, even the too-good-to-be-true story of the capture and rescue of Jessica Lynch [during the 2003 Iraqi invasion], have prompted little popular outcry against women's role in the war, and little evidence that the public is somehow less willing to tolerate their suffering than that of men. And while Lynndie England drew public attention and outrage for her role in the Abu Ghraib prison scandal, advocates of women in the military say critics have been on the lookout for any systemic failure of women to perform well in Iraq—and have found little to point to. Instead, just as the invasion of Panama and the Persian Gulf War led to reviews of women's role in the military—and expansions of the positions open to them—Iraq will likely prompt another reconsideration. Any increase in their combat role would improve women's opportunities at the top of the command structure, where their numbers are small today in part because of their lack of combat experience.

More important than how uniformed women and the public have reacted is how America's armed services have fared. After more than 30 years of experience with women in leadership positions and in the ranks, what may be most surprising is how little the rise of women has actually affected the American military. Make no mistake; the armed services have experienced enormous changes, including the incorporation of both devastating new killing technologies and more family-friendly personnel policies. But just as women's distinctive contribution to the forging of today's highly effective fighting force is hard to identify, so is it difficult to say what part they have played in enhancing some of the military's "softer" features.

Technological advances, new thinking from outside the military, changes in the attributes of senior leaders, and the demands of the all-volunteer force have resulted in adjustments in the way the military is led. Women as well as men have had to change. . . .

A History of Skepticism

Today's general acceptance of women on the battlefield is a far cry from the skepticism—and sometimes outright hostility— that greeted the opening of the services to women after the end of the Vietnam War. Faced with manpower shortages when the draft ended in 1973 and expecting that the Equal Rights Amendment would be enacted, Pentagon officials set aggressive goals for recruiting women and started changing the rules that governed the jobs female service members were allowed to do. American women already had a long military history, but it was a history that had largely seen them confined to separate branches such as the WAVES [Women Accepted for Volunteer Emergency Service] and WAAC [Women's Army Auxiliary Corps], which called on women to enlist during World War II in order to "free a man to fight." Now women were to be integrated into regular service units. Could they really carry heavy packs on their backs? What would happen if they got pregnant? Would military wives put up with their presence in the ranks?

A question posed in a 1976 study by the U.S. Army Research Institute for the Behavioral and Social Sciences provided a gauge of prevailing attitudes: "What percentage of women will it take to degrade unit performance?" But the results of a three-day field exercise with units ranging from all-male to 35 percent female, and a follow-up study the next year, surprised nearly everyone. "When properly trained and led, women are proving to be good soldiers in the field, as well as in garrison," the Army concluded. A research brief titled "Military Readiness: Women Are Not a Problem," published by RAND in 1997, showed that the tone had shifted a little in 20 years. It found that gender integration in military units "had a relatively small effect on readiness, cohesion, and morale," but that a unit's leadership, training, and workload had a much deeper influence. . . .

In the United States, one of the main complaints of critics is differing physical standards for men and women. (To get a perfect score on the Army fitness test, a 22-year-old man must do 75 push-ups, 80 sit-ups, and run two miles in 13 minutes. Women soldiers must do 46 push-ups, 80 sit-ups, and run two miles in 15:38.) The promotion system is another sore spot. Boards that meet each year to consider which officers from each service will be promoted make their decisions based on the information they find in a file about each candidate, including work history, training, honors, performance evaluations, any disciplinary action—often a photograph. They are also given equal opportunity goals, designed to ensure that the number of women and minorities promoted in each group of officers reflects that group's representation in the promotable pool. Such guidelines urge board members not to penalize candidates because they lack certain job experiences, such as combat assignments, if they were barred from such positions.

But race and gender are not the only concerns. The promotion boards are pulled in many other directions as well, needing to keep a balance between, say, helicopter and fixed-wing pilots. Most analyses find the promotion system to be widely accepted by men and women within the military.

For many of the women who entered the military in the 1970s and are senior officers today, it is simply the access to that merit system, the chance to succeed or fail based on their own performance without first being discounted by others and denied opportunities because of their gender, that may be the biggest change they have seen.

The Brass Ceiling

Despite that opportunity, and their larger numbers, women face a "brass ceiling," with only the thinnest representation at the highest ranks. The limited range of combat-related jobs open to women until the 1990s meant that many lack the experience that is highly valued in promotion decisions. At the same time, the arc of a military career is long, and because the service academies only opened their doors to women in 1976, the cohort of female officers with both those top credentials are only now in position to use them to help push their careers to the highest levels.

In the face of such institutional limits to advancement, it can be difficult to understand why so many women entered the military in the 1970s and '80s. Many say they did so because they wanted the chance to serve their country, just like men, and to explore interesting career paths. But there was something else. Vice Admiral [Ann E.] Rondeau, one of just five female officers with three stars currently serving in the U.S. military and frequently mentioned as a candidate to become the first four-star woman in the country's history, explains: "There were glass ceilings. There were prejudices. There were barriers. But . . . there was equal pay for equal work." . . .

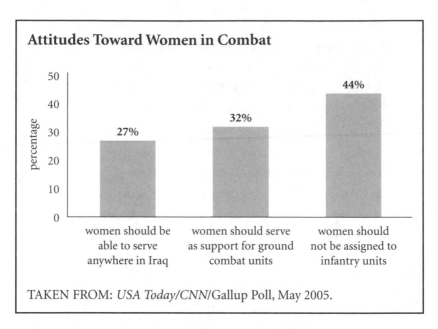

Attitudes Toward Women in Combat

TAKEN FROM: *USA Today/CNN/*Gallup Poll, May 2005.

A Traditional Culture

It is hard to find anyone, male or female, in or out of uniform, who would assert that the ascendance of women to leadership positions has fundamentally changed martial culture. "The military is still not just overwhelmingly male, but its ways of doing things are still very male," says Mady Segal, a sociology professor at the University of Maryland whose work focuses on women in the military. Top leaders go to the service academies, where traditional culture is reinforced. Even though about 20 percent of new students are women, they must make difficult adjustments. But perhaps more important in maintaining the military's ethos than tradition and machismo, haircuts and push-ups, is the fact that much of what the military does is determined by its well-defined mission to be ready, as the Army field manual puts it, "to fight and win the Nation's wars."

Successful women in the military are well aware of that basic fact, and many say they did not arrive with a desire to change the institution. "You are joining an institution that has doctrine, that has tradition, and you either appreciate it and come to love that aspect of the institution, or at some point you say, 'No, this really isn't where I want to be in life,' and you go back to civilian life," says Rear Admiral Michelle Howard, who graduated from the Naval Academy in 1982, a member of the third class to include women.

Retaining an All-Volunteer Force

The strength of that tradition does not mean that the organization has not changed since the 1970s. But while those changes—in management style, family-friendliness, and other areas—may be seen as a shift toward what management gums call a more "feminine" approach to leadership, they reflect other factors at work—most important, the demands of attracting, and retaining, the all-volunteer force. Younger people in all walks of life are less willing to sacrifice everything for their careers, and are more concerned with preserving their lives outside work. As in the corporate world, military leaders have recognized the need for policies to protect investments in careers and training with benefits for families, as well as for soldiers themselves. But the prospect of losing skilled professionals—in an organization that wants its leadership to be as diverse as its enlisted corps—is in some ways more troubling for the military. . . .

Female officers said their chances to perform and the recognition they received were "diminished by expectations that they are less capable," according to the study. Female officers reported "difficulties forming peer and mentor relationships," and said they "receive fewer career-enhancing assignments." They also cited a conflict between work demands and family responsibilities, and a lack of consensus on the appropriate role for women in the military. The female officers said sexual harassment leads to an uncomfortable working environment for women who are harassed, and they agreed that male fears of harassment charges had inhibited interactions between men and women.

Officers of both sexes cited the amount of time they spent away from their families and the enjoyment they got from their jobs as the most important factors influencing their decision about whether to leave the Army. But family issues appear to have a special effect on women officers. In the research institute study, time away from family was listed as the most important reason by 43 percent of women planning to leave, and 27 percent of men. One reason for the difference is that female officers are much more likely than their male peers to be married to another person in the military, who can't easily follow when a new posting comes along. Another study, conducted in 1997 by the Army Research Institute, found that 80 percent of male officers were married, but just 7 percent of them had wives in the military. Among female officers, 58 percent were married, and more than half of their spouses were also in the military. . . .

A Need for Women

Even [Elaine] Donnelly, perhaps the most outspoken conservative critic of the Pentagon's gender policies, doesn't directly call for a rollback of women's role in the military. As a practical matter, it is hard to see how the Army and other branches could be staffed without a significant complement of women—and some politicians in both parties are calling for an expansion of troop strength.

Does all this mean that it is only a matter of time until women are fully integrated into the armed services leadership? New technology, fresh attention to inclusive leadership styles, and societal attitudes all favor a greater role for women in the top ranks.

Deeper changes in military culture, however, are likely to be difficult. Along with the physiological fact that most women cannot develop the upper body strength thought to be needed in traditional warfare, general questions about their fitness for the most direct combat assignments remain. Lory Manning, of the Women's Research & Education Institute, says that the issue of women in combat will still be politically sensitive, but she expects it to be reexamined after the Iraq War. She singles out the "co-location rule," which prohibits women with noncombat jobs, such as medics and mechanics, from being based with combat units, as one that will likely be changed formally after the war. "Sheer necessity made it go away" in Iraq. But Manning does not foresee a sweeping removal of the remaining bans on direct combat.

The career of Erin Morgan, who graduated from West Point in May [2007] and is now a second lieutenant in the Army Intelligence Corps, is off to a promising start, with wide opportunities and the open doors that a degree from the academy can secure. But a few weeks before graduation, she said that women still do not have an easy time fitting in. "Soldiering is a masculine trait, something that separates the men from the women and the men from the boys," she says. "That is something that cadets still struggle with."

Amid the constant reminders of great warriors of the past embodied in statues and paintings at West Point, Morgan saw depictions of Douglas MacArthur, George Patton, Dwight Eisenhower, and other fabled generals. But she was only able to find one woman: Joan of Arc, whose image is part of the mess hall mural.

> *"America never consciously chose to send women into combat, but they are there now and in some cases are paying a tragic price."*

Women Are Not Prepared to Serve in Combat

Kelley Beaucar Vlahos

Women in combat positions are vulnerable to sexual assault and other noncombat-related injuries because they are not prepared to serve in combat, argues Kelley Beaucar Vlahos in the following viewpoint. Nevertheless, she claims, the demands of an all-volunteer force in Iraq and Afghanistan have forced women into combat roles. Under battle stress, Vlahos maintains, good men and women placed in close proximity sometimes engage in unprofessional behavior that threatens morale and combat readiness. As a result, she reasons, these women are paying a tragic price for their illegal integration into combat units. Vlahos is a Washington, D.C., journalist.

As you read, consider the following questions:

1. How has the number of women serving in the armed forces changed since Vietnam, in Vlahos's view?

Kelly Beaucar Vlahos, "Women at War," *American Conservative*, vol. 7, April 7, 2008, pp. 14–17.

2. According to the author, what threats do critics argue putting women into combat will pose?

3. In the author's opinion, what would happen in Iraq if Congress declared the combat zone off limits to women?

A high point of Kayla Williams's service as a noncommissioned Army officer in Iraq was receiving a commendation for her support on missions in Baghdad. Low points included getting molested by one of her own men and being asked to mock a naked Iraqi prisoner in an interrogation cage in Mosul.

Riding a line between woman and warrior, "bitch" and "slut," Williams, 31, was not alone. The [George W.] Bush administration's "long war" has forced the military to shock integrate more than 180,000 women into Iraq and Afghanistan over the last six years [between 2003 and 2008]. The consequences have been both impressive and ugly and do little to put to rest decades of debate over women in combat.

Critics say the rush to put women into combat-related roles for which they weren't trained has made them more vulnerable, exacerbated male-female tensions in theater [field of operations], and advanced a controversial policy while most of the country wasn't looking.

"We have large numbers of women who have been willing to come into the armed forces, who are willing to do jobs for which we have a shortage of young men," says one retired Army colonel, now in the private sector, who declined to be identified because of his ties to the defense community. "I think the women under these circumstances do the best they can."

A Clouded Story

Veterans who have spoken to TAC [*The American Conservative*] say most female soldiers have exceeded expectations. But the experience of the largest contingent of female soldiers in modern history is not unclouded. The rate of single motherhood among women on active duty is 14 percent, and nursing mothers are being deployed four months after giving birth. Reports of sexual assault are climbing, as are suicides and the number of women—now over 36,000—who have visited VA [Veterans Administration] hospitals since leaving the service. As of February [2008], 102 female soldiers had died in Iraq.

Meanwhile, the Army, which represents most women in theater, won't release figures on how many are evacuated from the field due to noncombat injuries, illness, or pregnancy.

"Whatever they are able to conceal or cover that's not attractive—whether it's unplanned pregnancy, rapes, whatever—everyone is prepared to pretend what is happening really isn't," says the retired colonel.

The drive to integrate women into every crevice of the military—the "ungendered vision" advocated by Duke law professor Madeleine Morris, a former assistant to [Bill] Clinton administration Army Secretary Togo West—has created turmoil in Washington since the 1970s. And since then the number of women in the armed forces has increased dramatically, from 7,000 in Vietnam (mostly medical personnel) to over 40,000 in the Persian Gulf War to one in seven of our troops in Iraq today.

Thanks to Clinton-era liberals—like former Representative Pat Schroeder and women-in-combat pioneers like Army Assistant Secretary Sara Lister, who was forced to resign in 1997 after she called the Marines "extremists"—new roles opened to women in the 1990s. Formerly all-male military academies and basic training programs turned co-ed. Today, tens of thousands of women are flying combat aircraft and serving as military police, gunners operating MK19 grenade launchers, interrogators, and prison guards.

The Reality of Women in Combat

Officially, women have not yet ventured into combat, held back by critics who argue that putting them into armored cavalry squadrons or rifle platoons will threaten unit cohesion, weaken standards, and increase injuries, hurting overall force strength. But advocates of full integration insist that women can hold their own on men's terms. Making them "legitimate" will help transform military culture and bolster unit cohesion.

These arguments are academic, for women are in combat today. While the Bush administration initially appeared less interested in integration than its predecessor, the decision to invade Iraq in 2003, the miscalculation of the subsequent insurgency and civil war, and the desire to wage a global terror war have made it impossible for the all-volunteer force to function without women in combat roles. Reality has taken over.

But if this and future administrations want to continue waging protracted asymmetrical wars with multiple fronts, wars in which everyone—not just combat troops and Marines—has to be on point, the negative consequences of shock integration will have to be acknowledged and addressed.

"In 2004, 2005, and probably in 2006, commanders were jockeying for resources," says retired Colonel Janice Karpinski. "There was this increase of women in a variety of positions they've never been in. They did very well. They were wounded, they had their limbs blown off, shot into the sky. They needed to be there, if [only] for their numbers. If we removed every female, you would have to have had a backwards draft."

Young men home from war are pragmatic about the women who served alongside them. They don't hesitate to tell of their bravery—the female Chinook pilot, for example, who flew night missions under fire to rescue teams in the mountains of Afghanistan—but they are blunt about the stories that

117

rarely make headlines: sexual mischief, the pretty specialist who left one day and never came back, the rumors of rape never confirmed.

Jason Hartley, who served as an infantry sergeant in Iraq from 2004 to 2005, says the way the military dealt with the new atmosphere created by integration was much like the execution of the war policy overall: confused, inconsistent, reactionary. "Everything gets f—ed up and broken. Then you step back and study it," says Hartley, who published *Just Another Soldier: A Year on the Ground in Iraq* when he returned from the war.

A Lack of Data

Studying the consequences of shock integration can be slippery. Grim anecdotes are abundant—but so too are tales of transcendence. There is a lack of hard data, as it is impossible to measure the number of illicit romances, the impact on a team when an affair turns sour, the lack of response when a woman asks for help, the women who are afraid to ask, the alcohol-fueled encounters, the sexual harassment, the male resentment toward female commanding officers.

"We've had six years to study this, but as far as I know, nobody is," says Kingsley Browne, a law professor at Wayne State University. Browne has written a book, *Co-Ed Combat: The New Evidence That Women Shouldn't Fight the Nation's Wars*, which pieces together interviews with soldiers and what little information has slipped into the public domain. "The military has consistently glossed over problems and denied them, denied access to information that could reveal problems," he says. "To a large extent it is in nobody's larger interest to reveal that information."

Spotty Coverage and Mythmaking

Media coverage has been spotty and safe, though most women in the military prefer to be left alone with their M16s and cigarettes rather than become subjects of iconic—or worse, pitying—stories about their sex. Television, where most people get their 30 seconds of war news a day, has avoided all but the most superficial discussions about women in combat and has reduced the narrative to three stories: those of Jessica Lynch, Lynndie England, and Janice Karpinski, whose sunken eyes betray a 30-year career that ended in disgrace. She characterizes her experience as losing ten rounds with the glass ceiling.

Lynch became, for a shining moment, the face of Operation Iraqi Freedom. She was also the military's first and last awkward attempt to spin the women-in-combat story for public consumption. A petite blonde teenager from a military family, Lynch was severely injured when her supply truck was ambushed by Iraqi fighters on March 23, 2003. Her best friend, Lori Piestewa, a single mother who left two toddlers behind, died from her injuries that day, the first woman killed in the war.

Yet the administration preferred a live hero to a dead one, and Piestewa became a sidebar while Lynch and her West Virginia family were used as patriotic props. Soon after her rescue by U.S. Special Forces, almost every angle of Lynch's daring resistance and rescue was disputed, even by Lynch herself, who testified before Congress last year [2007] that the government had engaged in mythmaking at her expense.

By the time photos surfaced showing Lynch cavorting topless with her fellow soldiers on base, she had been all used up.

The next time a female soldier penetrated the American consciousness she was holding a leash attached to an Iraqi detainee. Elfin and eerily detached, Lynndie England, 21, was pregnant by fellow reservist Charles Graner, the alleged mastermind of their military police company's notorious sex parties and the grotesque menagerie of photos that led to scandal in 2004. England and several other soldiers were shown abusing detainees at Abu Ghraib prison, posing them naked in pyramids, giving that infamous "thumbs up" alongside their corpses.

Graner, who allegedly manipulated England into staging all sorts of sex photos before and during their deployment, is still in jail. England is on parole, facing a future-crushing dishonorable discharge. She remains a curious example of women who attempted to fit in and went dangerously astray: In a 2006 interview with *Marie Claire*, the lifelong animal lover recalled how she and her fellow soldiers found humor in toying with animal carcasses in the desert.

The Highest Ranking Woman in Iraq

Karpinski, who was in charge of Abu Ghraib along with 14 other detention centers, was a brigadier general, the highest-ranking woman in Iraq when the scandal broke. "Not one of my units were trained to perform prison operations in a combat zone," she says. "None of them." She recalled one male commander's attitude: "Women made their own bed, let them lie in it."

Maintaining that the mistreatment of prisoners was sanctioned from the top, Karpinski says she was made a scapegoat, partly because she is a woman. She was demoted a year later. "They made me a pox on our history," says Karpinski, now an Army antagonist.

She notes that partisans in the old integration debate have been oddly quiet. "Where is the National Organization for Women? Where is Hillary Clinton? Where is Nancy Pelosi?" she asks, adding that the women who encouraged other women to "be all that you can be" are now abandoning them to the wolves. "When we have women who come back bruised mentally and physically and have nowhere to go, it's too late to say, 'We should have.' It needs to be done now. Not ten years from now."

The Pressures of the Pack

Women have different ways of dealing with the pressures of the pack and of battle stress, and the massive forward operating bases in Iraq have become petri dishes teeming with strange sexual dynamics and juvenile diversions.

"You got these women in huge, walled garrisons that are getting mortared all the time," says former Sergeant Rick Scavetta, 34, who served in both Iraq and Afghanistan before leaving the military in 2006, "not to mention you have large numbers of men, who aren't bad guys, not immoral or indecent, but you put men who've been in combat for a year in this small container and shake it up with IED [improvised explosive device] blasts and mortar blasts and it makes for a unique environment."

Another former Army sergeant who served in Afghanistan reports a similar scene. "You have a bunch of males on the base and a small female population. Then you get downtime. Then things start to happen. It's just like high school. Then you have females who ruin the reputation of the other females. It can be very debilitating."

Hartley describes a situation in which his quick reaction force was called up and found to be three men short. It was surmised that the missing soldiers were "hanging out with a chick who had a room right next to the staging area." "We left," he continued, "sans three dudes, including our 50-cal. gunner. It was bad."

In the 2005 scandal at Camp Bucca [a prison camp in Iraq], sergeants were accused of lending their rooms for sex parties and arranging mud-wrestling contests involving topless female prison guards.

Thanks in part to the behavior of a minority, says Bethany Kibler, 27, a noncommissioned officer in the Army reserves who spent a year in Iraq, women must fight doubly hard against shopworn stereotypes like the idea that they wield their sexuality to win special treatment or get pregnant to

Women Don't Belong in Combat

Women don't belong on warships, let alone in command of them. Women don't belong in the cockpits of fighter planes and bombers that can be shot down over enemy territory. Women don't belong on the front lines in any military capacity. . . .

I don't say this because I am a male chauvinist. I say it because I treasure and honor women.

Joseph Farah,
"No More Women Near Combat," WorldNetDaily.com,
November 7, 2003. www.wnd.com.

avoid service. This leads to "a sort of female hate." To overcome this, most women in the military act tough and tend to be judgmental of each other, she says. Many women feel compelled to keep up with the men, to act like their sisters. But in such permissive, stressful circumstances, that armor is easily breached.

Betrayal and Sexual Assault

Kayla Williams, who wrote proudly about her Iraq experience in *Love My Rifle More than You: Young and Female in the U.S. Army*, says that between the six- and eight-month mark of her 2003 deployment, "there was a general breakdown in military bearing and professionalism" among her team in the field. Fellow soldiers started flipping out; others got their kicks from telling rape jokes. Williams didn't care much when she was called a "bitch" in a heated moment, but she lost it when a fellow soldier tried to force her hand onto his penis in the dark. She reported the incident, and he was transferred. But the damage was lasting.

"I felt somehow betrayed," she admits and, conversely, "like I had somehow led . . . to this situation." She worried that because she had tried to be a pal, she may have sent the wrong signals. She eventually succumbed to being "the bitch" rather than "the slut," the dichotomy women say is the male code. "It was difficult and lonely," Williams says.

Sexual assault reports across the armed forces increased from 1,700 in 2004 to 2,947 in 2006, then dipped to 2,688 in 2007, according to the Sexual Assault Prevention and Response Office at the Pentagon. In the Central Command region, which includes Iraq, Afghanistan, and Kuwait, there were 206 reports in 2006 and 174 in 2007.

Anita Sanchez of the Miles Foundation, a nonprofit that has an arrangement with the Pentagon to provide immediate care to rape and assault victims in theater and also serves veterans stateside, says the government's official data seem "a bit low" in her experience.

"[The incidents] are going up significantly," she says, and not all are being reported because women still avoid coming forward. They expect the male leadership to close ranks around the accused, or they fear getting transferred or, worse, branded. She charges that "there are ongoing reservations about the DoD's [Department of Defense's] ability to collect, maintain, and analyze the data."

One former sergeant, who served in Iraq in a public affairs unit before leaving the military, says it is in the Army's best interest to "cover up" the ugliness. "They just don't want to admit it's a hostile environment against women," he says. Army officials flatly deny such charges.

Barbie and Matt Heavrin aren't sure. They were told their 21-year-old daughter was killed crossing the street on base in Iraq on April 4, 2006. They found out later, as the *Washington Post* recently reported, that their daughter, Private First Class Hannah Gunterman McKinney, a young mother herself, was killed when she fell out of a Humvee driven by Sergeant Damon Shell, who accidentally ran her over and left her mangled body in the road. The two had been drinking and having sex earlier that evening.

The Problem of Proximity

Elaine Donnelly of the Center for Military Readiness doesn't buy the idea that poor leadership and training and inconsistent boundaries are to blame for today's problems. She insists the troubles stem from throwing men and women so close together in the first place. She would start rehabilitating the situation by insisting that the Army stop illegally collocating women in support brigades with all-male combat units in the field—a practice Army officials deny is even happening.

"We have to figure out what is the best way, the most constructive way, to have a co-ed military," says Donnelly. "To the greatest extent possible you have to acknowledge that sexuality does matter."

"Women have done very well," she adds, "but it's very disturbing that the signs of trouble and problems have not been given objective review. Our Congress has turned its back. The Pentagon has made excuses."

Men and women home from the war acknowledge that there are many questions from the old co-ed combat debate still unresolved, despite years of experimentation.

Williams, who has traded her rifle for a graduate program at American University, warns against knee-jerk reactions either way. If Congress were to declare the entire combat zone off-limits to women, for example, the Army in Iraq would suddenly become "15 percent undeployable," she says.

Shock integration happened when the administration decided to wage a war in Iraq on top of an increasingly complex operation in Afghanistan. And now women in unprecedented combat roles have become essential to sustaining force strength overseas. . . .

America never consciously chose to send women into combat, but they are there now and in some cases are paying a tragic price.

> "Recruiting comes down to a numbers
> game, and the numbers reveal the chal-
> lenge that the Army faces as it tries to
> expand and sustain a wartime force."

U.S. Armed Forces Recruiters Meet Serious Challenges

James Kitfield

When the draft ended, no one anticipated that the United States would be fighting another war that would last for years, claims James Kitfield in the following viewpoint. The numbers needed to fight in Iraq and Afghanistan, however, make meeting recruitment goals very challenging, he asserts. Those who meet the target age group often fail to meet the military's standards, Kitfield maintains. In fact, he reports, recruiters often work up to seventy-five-hour workweeks just to recruit two enlistees each month. Kitfield is the national security and foreign affairs correspondent for National Journal.

As you read, consider the following questions:

1. In Kitfield's view, where do recruiters ply their trade?

2. What do recruiters make sure enlistees understand, in the author's opinion?

3. According to the author what has been the army's controversial answer to the need for more recruits?

Houston—As far as Capt. Antonio Hernandez is concerned, the most important front for a wartime Army can be seen from this small recruiting station tucked in a strip mall in Friendswood, Texas. On this morning, Hernandez, a company commander in the Army's Houston recruiting battalion, is checking in on one of his teams and talking to a chunky young man with the patchy whiskers of someone not yet accustomed to shaving regularly. Sitting beside the potential recruit is his teenage girlfriend, feet tucked up on the chair and knees to her chin.

"So how'd you do on the aptitude test?" Hernandez asks.

The young man responds that he got a relatively high score on the military's standard aptitude test, but he is worried that his height-to-weight ratio and body-fat level are outside Army standards.

"Don't worry, you don't look too bad," Hernandez assures him. "You'll be huffing and puffing at first, but by the time you get through basic, you'll run a couple of miles without breaking a sweat."

"I hope so," the young man says, seeming to recall the language of a recruiting brochure as he adds, "I definitely want to maximize my physical potential."

Recruiting is a delicate dance and one with little modern precedent: an army of uniformed recruiters, scouring the countryside looking for young men and women to fight an all-volunteer war. Part pitchmen and part guidance counselors, recruiters ply their trade at NASCAR events and rodeos, at auto shows and drag races, at high school football games and spring-break parties, and even on college campuses. You can find them wherever America's youth gather, practicing what Hernandez calls the "science of sales balanced with the art of influencing someone to make a life-changing decision." Be part of something bigger than yourself. Use the modern-day GI Bill to go to college. Secure a good job when you get out. Defend your country against all enemies. Maximize your potential.

Here in the heartland, that message resonates powerfully. The Houston recruiting battalion—whose 180 recruiters have to work a territory that spans 39,000 square miles and includes 360 high schools, 59 colleges, and 47 recruiting stations—nearly always makes its goal. In recent years the battalion has put an average of 3,200 fresh recruits "into boots" annually. When recruiters eat in crowded restaurants, they often find that someone has paid for their meals by the time they finish. People walk up to shake their hands and to thank them for their service. Strangers applaud them in airports.

"Texas is plain patriotic, and its support for the military is beyond anything that I've seen," said Lt. Col. Troy Reeves, commander of the Houston recruiting battalion.

Yet persuading young Americans raised on McDonald's supersized meals and Xbox video games to join a wartime Army is anything but easy. When its founders crafted the all-volunteer military in the 1970s, they never anticipated that it would be sent off to fight a war lasting years. At that time, even deploying the force required a major call-up of reserves, and the all-volunteer force was viewed as merely the vanguard of a mass-mobilization army augmented by the draft. Today, the all-volunteer Army is in its fifth year of combat with no end to fighting in sight.

"We make sure enlistees understand that there is a good possibility that they will deploy to Iraq and Afghanistan, and when I'm asked about that my reply is that we didn't start this war," Hernandez said. "Al Qaeda attacked us on U.S. soil, and we're fighting them over there so we don't have to fight them here. I also point out that freedom isn't free. The bottom line is that if my recruiters don't put people into uniform, the Army is not going to be able to put platoons in the field to do the fighting. So we all believe in what we're doing here."

The science of recruiting comes down to a numbers game, and the numbers reveal the challenge that the Army faces as it tries to expand and sustain a wartime force. Of the primary target audience of 17- to 24-year-olds, only about three in 10 are high school graduates who can also meet the service's mental, physical, and moral standards. Yet the Army remains a voracious consumer of manpower, needing 80,000 recruits in 2007 just to maintain its current size. That figure is more than twice the number of new men and women that any of the other armed services need. And this number is slated to increase to 84,000 in fiscal 2008, as the Army attempts over several years to expand its total size by 65,000 soldiers. Meanwhile, the "propensity" of American youth to join the military, as measured by annual surveys given to high school students, is down somewhat in recent years, and more than 65 percent of graduating seniors now opt to attend college rather than to join the military.

"The trends in terms of the obesity and misdemeanor convictions are also not in our favor, because kids are getting heavier, and they are more likely to get arrested in this post-Columbine era for things they would have just been sent home from school for in the past," said Col. Don Bartholomew, referring to the 1999 shootings at Columbine High School in Colorado. "So the nature of demographics dictated that we were going to have a very tough time if we didn't adjust our standards," Bartholomew, the head of marketing and strategic communications at Army Accessions Command at Fort Monroe, Va., continued. "We had to expand the pool of potential recruits."

The Army's controversial answer was to grant "waivers" of its standards to 15 percent of its recruits in fiscal 2006. About half of those (7.7 percent) were given "moral waivers" because of criminal records (7,202 for misdemeanors and more than 1,000 for more-serious crimes, most of them felonies), according to the Army Recruiting Command. An additional 6.3 percent were given "medical waivers." The remaining 1 percent (1,063 recruits) were given "drug and alcohol" waivers. According to the Center for Strategic and Budgetary Assessments [CSBA], a defense think tank in Washington, high school graduates made up 82 percent of the 2006 enlistment class (not including those with an "equivalent," or GED, degree); that's below the Army's benchmark of 90 percent and the lowest rate since 1981. The number of recruits scoring above the 50th percentile on the military aptitude test was 61 percent, the lowest proportion since 1985, according to the CSBA. The Army also raised its age limit for recruits to 42 and altered the basic training regime with an eye toward failing fewer trainees. As a result, the basic training graduation rate rose from 82 percent in 2005 to 94 percent in 2006.

"The numbers indicate that moral waivers in the Army have quadrupled over the last decade," said CSBA Executive Director Andrew Krepinevich, a retired Army lieutenant colonel. "They are allowing significantly more high school dropouts and felons into uniform; they appear to be lowering standards in basic training; and if it wasn't for recruits over the age of 35, the Army would have come close to missing its recruiting goal last year. That adds up to a pretty dicey picture."

For Army recruiters, the numbers game breaks down like this: Even a talented recruiter with natural sales skills will need to make initial contact with a minimum of 40 potential recruits each month. Through follow-up phone calls and e-mails, they must somehow persuade 24 of those prospects to make an appointment to hear the Army's telephone pitch about enlistment bonuses, which average $20,000 but can reach $40,000 in some cases, and Army College Fund guarantees, which average $37,000 but can climb higher depending on the military specialty chosen. Of that group, 16 must be sufficiently interested to come to a recruiting station for the full pitch; at least four of those eventually need to take the aptitude and physical tests to confirm that they are qualified to join. Because at the end of each month of typically 65- to 75-hour workweeks, each and every one of the service's 8,425 recruiters must put two enlistees into boots for the numbers to add up for the Army. Or, as a recruiter will tell you, "It's all about the contracts."

The majority of recruiters today are combat veterans who will return to operational units and lead the same recruits they sign up. And at some point during all of their face time with the youth of America and their families, coaches, and high school guidance counselors, those recruiters seem to stop worrying about the quality of the nation's new warrior class. For every waiver statistic, they have a personal anecdote about the 39-year-old mother of six who lost 40 pounds so she could join the Army, or the surgeon who enlisted just to do his part as a medic, or the "felon" whose crime was playing with matches as a youngster and accidentally burning down his neighbor's toolshed.

The statistic that matters most, these recruiters will tell you, is the one that tends to be overlooked. "This generation we're recruiting right now, you've got to realize that these kids are joining the Army of a nation at war," said Sergeant 1st Class Charles Colbert, commander of a small recruiting station in Friendswood, Texas. "Damn, how can your hat not be off to someone like that?"

> *"New [recruiting] policies [are] creating a lower-quality officer corps and the Pentagon [is] pulling out ever more stops and sinking to new lows to recruit and train troops."*

U.S. Armed Forces Recruiting Tactics Are Unethical

Nick Turse

To meet its recruiting goals, the military is reducing its standards, argues Nick Turse in the following viewpoint. As opposition to the war in Iraq grows, the numbers willing to enlist decrease, as does the quality of recruits, he reasons. Due to the increasing number of moral waivers, the armed forces are recruiting enlistees with criminal records, Turse asserts, in some cases even seeking them out. Some of these recruits are gang members who threaten the cohesion necessary in combat, he claims. Turse works in the Department of Epidemiology at Columbia University.

As you read, consider the following questions:

1. According to Turse, why is the story of Steven Green instructive?

2. In the author's opinion, how are neo-Nazis using their Army experience?

3. What does the author mean by a new all-volunteer generation of UUUUs?

After falling short of its goals last year [in 2005], military recruiting in 2006 has been marked by upbeat pronouncements from Defense Secretary Donald Rumsfeld, claims of success by the White House, and a spate of recent press reports touting the military's achievement of its woman- and manpower goals.

A Fundamental Transformation

But the armed forces have met with success only through a fundamental transformation, and not the transformation of the military—that "co-evolution of concepts, processes, organizations and technology" that Rumsfeld is always talking about either.

While the secretary of defense's long-standing goal of transforming the planet's most powerful military into its highest-tech, most agile, most futuristic fighting force has, in the words of the *Washington Post*'s David Von Drehle, "melted away," the very makeup of the armed forces has been mutating before our collective eyes under the pressure of the war in Iraq. This actual transformation has been reported, but only in scattered articles on the new recruitment landscape in America.

Last year, despite NASCAR, professional bull-riding and Arena Football sponsorships, popular video games that doubled as recruiting tools, TV commercials dripping with seductive scenes of military glory, a "joint marketing communications and market research and studies" program designed to attract, among others, dropouts and those with criminal records for military service, and at least $16,000 in promotional costs for each soldier it managed to sign up, the U.S. military failed to meet its recruiting goals.

This year, those methods have been pumped up and taken over the top in several critical areas that make the old Army ad tagline, "Be All You Can Be," into material for late-night TV punch lines of the future.

Opening the Door

In 2004, the Pentagon published a "Moral Waiver Study," whose seemingly benign goal was "to better define relationships between pre-Service behaviors and subsequent Service success." That turned out to mean opening more recruitment doors to potential enlistees with criminal records.

In February, the *Baltimore Sun* wrote that there was "a significant increase in the number of recruits with what the Army terms 'serious criminal misconduct' in their background"—a category that included "aggravated assault, robbery, vehicular manslaughter, receiving stolen property and making terrorist threats." From 2004 to 2005, the number of those recruits rose by more than 54 percent, while alcohol and illegal drug waivers, reversing a four-year decline, increased by more than 13 percent.

In June, the *Chicago Sun-Times* reported that, under pressure to fill the ranks, the Army had been allowing into its ranks increasing numbers of "recruits convicted of misdemeanor crimes, according to experts and military records." In fact, as the military's own data indicated, "the percentage of recruits entering the Army with waivers for misdemeanors and medical problems has more than doubled since 2001."

One beneficiary of the Army's new moral-waiver policies gained a certain prominence this summer. After Steven Green, who served in the 101st Airborne Division, was charged in a rape and quadruple murder in Mahmudiyah, Iraq, it was disclosed that he had been "a high school dropout from a broken home who enlisted to get some direction in his life, yet was sent home early because of an antisocial personality disorder."

Recently, Eli Flyer, a former Pentagon senior military analyst and specialist on the relationship between military recruiting and military misconduct, told *Harper's* magazine that Green had "enlisted with a moral waiver for at least two drug- or alcohol-related offenses. He committed a third alcohol-related offense just before enlistment, which led to jail time, although this offense may not have been known to the Army when he enlisted."

Trolling for Ex-Cons

With Green in jail awaiting trial, the *Houston Chronicle* reported in August that Army recruiters were trolling around the outskirts of a Dallas-area job fair for ex-convicts.

"We're looking for high school graduates with no more than one felony on their record," one recruiter said.

The Army has even looked behind prison bars for fill-in recruits—in one reported case, they went to a "youth prison" in Ogden, Utah. Although Steven Price had asked to see a recruiter while still incarcerated, he was "barely 17 when he enlisted last January" and his divorced parents say "recruiters used false promises and forged documents to enlist him."

While confusion exists about whether the boy's mother actually signed a parental consent form allowing her son to enlist, his "father apparently wasn't even at the signing, but his name is on the form too."

Enlisting Gang Members

Law enforcement officials report that the military is now "allowing more applicants with gang tattoos," the *Chicago Sun-Times* reports, "because they are under the gun to keep enlistment up." They also note that "gang activity may be rising among soldiers." The paper was provided with "photos of military buildings and equipment in Iraq that were vandalized with graffiti of gangs based in Chicago, Los Angeles and other cities."

Last month, the *Sun-Times* reported that a gang member facing federal charges of murder and robbery enlisted in the Marine Corps "while he was free on bond—and was preparing to ship out to boot camp when Marine officials recently discovered he was under indictment." While this recruit was eventually booted from the Corps, a Milwaukee police detective and Army veteran, who serves on the federal drug and gang task force that arrested the would-be Marine, noted that other "gang-bangers are going over to Iraq and sending weapons back . . . gang members are getting access to military training and weapons."

Earlier this year, it was reported that an expected transfer of 10,000 to 20,000 troops to Fort Bliss, Texas, caused FBI and local law enforcement to fear a turf war between "members of the Folk Nation gang . . . (and) a criminal group that is already well-established in the area, Barrio Azteca." The *New York Sun* wrote that, according to one FBI agent, "Folk Nation, which was founded in Chicago and includes several branches using the name Gangster Disciples, has gained a foothold in the Army."

Recruiting Extremists

Another type of gang member has also begun to proliferate within the military, evidently thanks to lowered recruitment standards and an increasing tendency of recruiters to look the other way. In July, a study by the Southern Poverty Law Center, which tracks racist and right-wing militia groups, found that because of pressing manpower concerns, "large numbers of neo-Nazis and skinhead extremists" are now serving in the military. "Recruiters are knowingly allowing neo-Nazis and white supremacists to join the armed forces, and commanders don't remove them from the military even after we positively

The Risks of Moral Waivers

The U.S. military is opening itself up to potential trouble by accepting more recruits with criminal records. . . .

There are risks in granting too many moral waivers. It could lead to more discipline problems in the ranks, and it could make military service less attractive to law-abiding citizens if they believe they will be in the company of former criminals.

Arizona Daily Star,
"Vigilance Needed as Military Eases Recruiting Rules,"
February 17, 2007. www.azstarnet.com.

identify them as extremists or gang members," said Scott Barfield, a Defense Department investigator quoted in the report.

The *New York Times* noted that the neo-Nazi magazine *Resistance* is actually recruiting for the U.S. military, urging "skinheads to join the Army and insist on being assigned to light infantry units." As the magazine explained, "The coming race war and the ethnic cleansing to follow will be very much an infantryman's war. . . . It will be house-to-house . . . until your town or city is cleared and the alien races are driven into the countryside where they can be hunted down and 'cleansed.'"

Apparently, the recruiting push has worked. Barfield reported that he and other investigators have identified a network of neo-Nazi active-duty Army and Marine personnel spread across five military installations in five states. "They're communicating with each other about weapons, about recruiting, about keeping their identities secret, about organizing within the military," he said.

Little wonder that Aryan Nation graffiti is now apparently competing for space with American inner-city gang graffiti in Iraq.

The UUUUs

In the latter half of the Vietnam War, the U.S. military started to crumble from within and American troops began scrawling "UUUU" on their helmet liners—an abbreviation that stood for "the unwilling, led by the unqualified, doing the unnecessary for the ungrateful."

With a growing majority of Americans opposed to the war in Iraq and even ardent hawks refusing to enlist in droves, new policies creating a lower-quality officer corps and the Pentagon pulling out ever more stops and sinking to new lows to recruit and train troops, a new all-volunteer generation of UUUUs may emerge—the underachieving, unable, unexceptional, unintelligent, unsound, unhinged, unacceptable, unhealthy, undesirable, unloved, and uncivil—all led by the unqualified, doing the unnecessary for the ungrateful.

Current practices suggest this may well be the force of the future. It certainly isn't the new military Rumsfeld's been promising all these years, but there's no denying the depth of the transformation.

Periodical Bibliography

The following articles have been selected to supplement the diverse views presented in this chapter.

American Civil Liberties Union — *Soldiers of Misfortune: Abusive U.S. Military Recruitment and Failure to Protect Child Soldiers*, May 13, 2008. www.aclu.org.

Bryan Bender — "Army Recruits with Diplomas Hit 25-Year Low," *Boston Globe*, January 23, 2008.

Kristin Henderson — "Women in Combat," Military.com, March 11, 2008.

Lawrence J. Korb — "The State of America's Ground Forces," Center for American Progress, April 16, 2008. www.americanprogress.org.

Allen McDuffee — "Dollar-Driven Recruiting," *Nation*, May 16, 2008.

Dana Milbank — "Sorry We Asked, Sorry You Told," *Washington Post*, July 24, 2008.

Taryn McCall Runk — "Feminists in the Military: Is Armed Service Compatible with Feminism?" *off our backs*, February 2006.

Thom Shanker — "'Don't Ask, Don't Tell' Hits Women Much More," *New York Times*, June 23, 2008.

Rachel L. Swarns — "Commanding a New Role for Women in the Military," *New York Times*, June 30, 2008.

Leonard Wong and Stephen Gerras — "All-Volunteer Army: An Ongoing Experiment," *USA Today*, June 25, 2008.

OPPOSING
VIEWPOINTS®
SERIES

CHAPTER 3

How Should Armed Forces Resources Be Managed?

Chapter Preface

As World War II drew to a close, Allied forces firebombed Dresden, Germany, killing an estimated 150,000 civilians. Military leaders at the time believed that bombing civilian areas would demoralize the population and therefore hasten surrender. U.S. president Harry Truman authorized the atomic bombing of Hiroshima, Japan, on August 6, 1945, and Nagasaki, Japan, on August 9, which resulted in the death of at least 250,000 people, many of whom were civilians. Military leaders believed that the bombs dropped on these Japanese cities were necessary to hasten surrender and therefore significantly reduced the number of Allied casualties they believed would result from an invasion of Japan. Those who believe that targeting civilians to spare combatants is sometimes necessary often cite these incidents to support their position. This reasoning, however, is subject to dispute and is one of several controversies in the debate concerning how armed forces resources should be used.

Opponents argue that targeting civilians to reduce one's own casualties is immoral and not supported by just war theory. Critics of this policy assert that the bombings of Dresden, Hiroshima, and Nagasaki were, in fact, war crimes. Targeting civilians is the rationale of terrorists, they maintain. In a 2002 article in *Atlantic Monthly*, Stuart Taylor Jr. quotes history professor Philip Bobbitt of the University of Texas Law School: "The terrorist does not reluctantly accept the accidental killings that accompany warfare; his whole point is to kill ordinary people in order to make them fearful. If we make targeting civilians lawful, we turn our armed forces into terrorists." Moreover, critics claim that intentionally targeting civilians does not work. Instead of demoralizing a civilian population, it has the opposite effect, appearing to stiffen their resolve—even in support of oppressive governments.

Those who support the targeting of civilians to save combatants argue that governments have a moral obligation to act in self-defense on behalf of their citizens. "Morally," claims objectivist scholar Onkar Ghate in a January 18, 2002, editorial republished on the Ayn Rand Web site, "the U.S. government must destroy our aggressors by whatever means are necessary and minimize U.S. casualties in the process." To achieve victory and minimize one's own casualties may require the deliberate targeting of civilians to "cripple [the aggressor nation's] economic production and/or break its will," as the Allies did by bombing Dresden, Hiroshima, and Nagasaki in World War II, Ghate maintains. In answer to claims that targeting civilians is monstrous, Ghate asserts, "The responsibility for all deaths in war lies with the aggressor who initiates force, not with those who defend themselves." In fact, Ghate reasons, truly innocent citizens will understand the right of free nations to "bomb their countries and destroy their governments—even if this jeopardizes their own lives."

The controversy over the targeting of civilians remains heated. The rhetoric used by those on both sides of this debate is reflective of other controversies explored by the authors in the following chapter. In the eyes of many commentators, the war on terror has changed the way armed forces are to be managed, and these changes will undoubtedly have an impact on attitudes toward civilian casualties.

> "We must institutionalize the lessons
> learned and capabilities honed from
> the ongoing conflicts."

The United States Should Prepare Its Armed Forces to Fight Current Conflicts

Robert M. Gates

Focusing on strategies that meet the goals of current conflicts is the best use of military resources, argues Robert M. Gates in the following viewpoint. Small forces of insurgents, guerrillas, and terrorists are the nation's most likely threats, he maintains. Therefore, Gates asserts, weapons programs that respond to these threats are more relevant than programs designed to meet the unlikely threat of larger, conventional militaries. The United States' primary goal should be to win the war in which it is engaged, he maintains. Secretary of Defense Gates served as Director of Central Intelligence under President George H.W. Bush.

As you read, consider the following questions:

1. According to Gates, why is he not the best person to speak at a conference titled "The Military Beyond Iraq"?

Robert M. Gates, "Remarks to the Heritage Foundation," in U.S. Department of Defense Speeches, May 13, 2008.

2. Why does Gates assert that the inclination toward "Next-War-itis" is understandable?

3. In the author's view, why are the Air Force and the Navy America's main strategic deterrent?

I appreciate the opportunity . . . to share some observations about the state of America's military.

For starters, I should note that, despite my job description, I may not actually be the best person to speak at a conference titled "The Military Beyond Iraq." I say this because for much of the past year [2008], I've been trying to concentrate the minds and energies of the defense establishment on the current needs and current conflicts. In short, to ensure that all parts of the Defense Department are, in fact, at war. . . .

Getting the Present Right

In my view, America's key asymmetric advantage is our people. And getting the present right when it comes to care of our men and women in uniform will go a long way towards making sure we have the kind of force we need in the future.

I use these examples as an introduction to a wider point. There is a good deal of debate and discussion—within the military, the Congress, and elsewhere—about whether we are putting too much emphasis on current demands—in particular, Iraq. And whether this emphasis is creating too much risk in other areas, such as:

- Preparing for potential future conflicts;

- Being able to handle a contingency elsewhere in the world; and

- Overstressing the ground forces, in particular the Army.

Much of what we are talking about is a matter of balancing risk: today's demands versus tomorrow's contingencies; irregular and asymmetric threats versus conventional threats. As the world's remaining superpower, we have to be able to dissuade, deter, and, if necessary, respond to challenges across the spectrum.

The Problem of Next-War-itis

Nonetheless, I have noticed too much of a tendency towards what might be called "Next-War-itis"—the propensity of much of the defense establishment to be in favor of what might be needed in a future conflict. This inclination is understandable, given the dominant role the Cold War had in shaping America's peacetime military, where the United States constantly strove to either keep up with or get ahead of another superpower adversary.

And, certainly, one cannot predict the future with any certainty. Soon after 1900, Winston Churchill said that he could not foresee any "collision of interests" with Germany. In the 1920s, as the Chancellor of the Exchequer, he said that there wasn't the "slightest chance" of war with Japan in his lifetime. Today, rising and resurgent powers with new wealth and ambition are pursuing military modernization programs. They must be watched closely and hedged against.

But in a world of finite knowledge and limited resources, where we have to make choices and set priorities, it makes sense to lean toward the most likely and lethal scenarios for our military. And it is hard to conceive of any country confronting the United States directly in conventional terms—ship to ship, fighter to fighter, tank to tank—for some time to come. The record of the past quarter century is clear: the Soviets in Afghanistan, the Israelis in Lebanon, the United States in Somalia, Afghanistan, and Iraq. Smaller, irregular forces—insurgents, guerrillas, terrorists—will find ways, as they always have, to frustrate and neutralize the advantages of larger, regular militaries. And even nation-states will try to exploit our perceived vulnerabilities in an asymmetric way, rather than play to our inherent strengths.

The Capabilities We Will Need

Overall, the kinds of capabilities we will most likely need in the years ahead will often resemble the kinds of capabilities we need today.

The implication, particularly for America's ground forces, means we must institutionalize the lessons learned and capabilities honed from the ongoing conflicts. Many of these skills and tasks used to be the province of the Special Forces, but now are a core of the Army and Marine Corps as a whole. For example, at West Point . . . , I told the cadets that the most important assignment in their careers may not necessarily be commanding U.S. soldiers, but advising or mentoring the troops of other nations. What we must guard against is the kind of backsliding that has occurred in the past, where if nature takes it course, these kinds of capabilities—that is counterinsurgency—tend to wither on the vine.

There is a history here. During the 1980s, a Princeton graduate student noted in his dissertation that, about a decade after the fall of Saigon, the Army's 10-month staff college assigned 30 hours—about four days—for what is now called low-intensity conflict. This was about the same as what the Air Force was teaching at the time. That grad student was then Army Major David Petraeus.

Going forward we must find, retain, and promote the right people—at all ranks, whether they wear stripes, bars, or stars—and put them in the right positions to see that the lessons learned in recent combat become rooted in the institutional culture. Similarly, we shouldn't let personnel policies that were developed in peacetime hurt our wartime performance.

For years to come, the Air Force and the Navy will be America's main strategic deterrent. We need to modernize our aging inventory of aircraft, and build out a fleet of ships that right now is the smallest we've had since the late 1930s. These forces provide the strategic flexibility we need to deter, and if necessary, respond to other competitors. The American people

A New Manual

A new manual on counterinsurgency coauthored by the man ... in charge of the war in Iraq, General David Petraeus, overturns the notion that America doesn't "do nation-building". Counterinsurgency, it says, is "armed social work". It requires more brain than brawn, more patience than aggression. The model soldier should be less science-fiction Terminator and more intellectual for "the graduate level of war", preferably a linguist, with a sense of history and anthropology.

Economist,
"Brains, Not Bullets: Armies of the Future,"
October 25, 2007.

have been generous when it comes to funding their Armed Forces over the past seven years, and they are likely to be supportive in the future. What we should expect, though, is a heightened level of scrutiny in the Congress, and by the public, for how this money is being spent—particularly when supplemental war funds are no longer available for modernization purposes.

Procurement and Global Risk

Two points on the subject of procurement:

First, I believe that any major weapons program, in order to remain viable, will have to show some utility and relevance to the kind of irregular campaigns that, as I mentioned, are most likely to engage America's military in the coming decades. In Texas, I had an opportunity to see a demonstration of the parts of the Army's Future Combat Systems [FCS] that have moved from the drawing board to reality. A program like FCS—whose total cost could exceed $200 billion if completely built out—must continue to demonstrate its value for the types of irregular challenges we will face, as well as for full-spectrum warfare. Second, I would stress that the perennial procurement cycle—going back many decades—of adding layer upon layer of cost and complexity onto fewer and fewer platforms that take longer and longer to build must come to an end.

Without a fundamental change in this dynamic, it will be difficult to sustain support for these kinds of weapons programs in the future.

A few words about global risk—the threats we face elsewhere in the world while America's ground forces are concentrated on Iraq.

This is an understandable concern. I remember being a second lieutenant at Whiteman Air Force Base in the late 1960s. There I caught a glimpse of the impact of the Vietnam War on America's overall strategic strength: White-haired lieutenant colonels were being reassigned to Southeast Asia to make up for our pilot losses there. Some people have made similar comparisons to the impact of Iraq on the Army.

Today's strategic context is completely different. While America's military was being bled in Vietnam, a superpower with vast fleets of tanks, bombers, fighters, and nuclear weapons was poised to overrun Western Europe—then the central theater [field of operations] in that era's long twilight struggle. Not so today.

It is true that we would be hard-pressed to launch a major conventional ground operation elsewhere in the world at this time—but where would we sensibly do that? The United States has ample and untapped combat power in our naval and air forces, with the capacity to defeat any—repeat, any—adversary who committed an act of aggression—whether in the Persian Gulf, on the Korean Peninsula, or in the Straits of Taiwan. There is a risk—but a prudent and manageable one.

Easing the Strain

The last point I'd like to address is the strain placed on our ground forces, especially the Army.

Along with Fort Bliss, I've visited a number of other military installations over the past year, including Fort Hood and Camp Pendleton—the largest Army and Marine bases respectively. It is a difficult thing to look a family member in the eye whose father or son or daughter is being deployed again—sometimes on a second or third tour. And it's even harder to do with the families of those who have been killed or wounded.

This is the second longest war in American history since our Revolution, and the first to be fought with an all-volunteer force since independence. To be sure the stress is real. There are metrics that need to be watched—such as the number of waivers granted to new recruits, suicides, as well as incidents of divorce and other signs of wear on military families.

There are a number of measures under way and trends that should ease the strain on this small sliver of our population who have borne the burden of this conflict:

- More and better programs to improve the quality of life for soldiers and their families;

- The ground forces are growing by more than 90,000 over the next five years—with a bigger rotational pool of troops and units, individual soldiers and Marines will deploy less frequently; and

- U.S. force levels in Iraq will decline over time—the debate taking place is mostly over the pacing.

As I mentioned before, the discussion about the stress on the Army today is informed by the Vietnam experience—and the terrible shape of the service afterwards, where there was a loss of nearly a generation of NCO [noncommissioned officer] leadership and rampant discipline problems. So far, none of those ailments are present today.

Overall, our service men and women and their families have shown extraordinary resilience. Morale is high, as is recruiting and retention—particularly among units either in or just returning from Iraq and Afghanistan. Soldier for soldier, unit for unit, the Army is the best trained, best led, and best equipped it has ever been—skilled and experienced in the arduous complexities of irregular warfare.

But there is a more fundamental point that I will close with—and again, historical perspective is important. It is impossible to separate discussions of the "broken" Army following Vietnam—a conscription army—from the ultimate result of that conflict. At a congressional hearing last year, General Jack Keane, former Vice Chief of Staff of the Army, recounted the profound damage done to the Service's "fiber and soul" by the reality of defeat in that war.

The risk of overextending the Army is real. But I believe the risk is far greater—to that institution, as well as to our country if we were to fail in Iraq. That is the war we are in. That is the war we must win.

> *"Relying on the experience in just one kind of conflict . . . carries the dangerous potential to have the nation learn the harsh lessons of defeat on tomorrow's battlefields."*

The United States Should Prepare Its Armed Forces for a Variety of Conflicts

Charles J. Dunlap Jr.

Preparing the armed forces for ongoing conflicts alone is dangerous, claims Charles J. Dunlap Jr. in the following viewpoint. The notion that most U.S. soldiers should be trained as social workers and civil engineers wrongly assumes that future conflicts will be like those in Iraq and Afghanistan, he maintains. The United States could survive losing these wars, but the price of losing a traditional, conventional war will be devastating, Dunlap reasons. The United States should therefore invest in technology that will help soldiers fight a wide range of conflicts, he concludes. Dunlap is Deputy Judge Advocate General in the U.S. Air Force.

Charles J. Dunlap Jr., "Forget the Lessons of Iraq," *Armed Forces Journal*, vol. 146, January 1, 2009, p. 12. Copyright © 2009 Armed Forces Journal. Reproduced by permission.

As you read, consider the following questions:

1. Why does Dunlap caution against making assumptions about the lessons of Iraq?

2. Despite the military success of 2007 and 2008, how do the American people feel about "Iraq-style" operations, according to Dunlap?

3. In the author's view, what vital lesson of "the Long War" has been overlooked? ·

Among defense intelligentsia, there are few mantras more chic than that which claims the U.S. military "forgot the lessons of Vietnam." Had it not done so, received wisdom insists, America's armed forces would not have struggled in Iraq for so long. Powerful adherents to this theory have spawned a follow-on analog, that we must not "forget the lessons of Iraq."

Unfortunately, some of the key lessons these enthusiasts believe should be learned are the wrong ones, and these mistaken ideas are causing America's military to be altered in ways that may prove troubling as the U.S. faces an increasingly complex and dangerous range of security threats.

Indeed, the devotees of the forgot-the-lessons-of-Vietnam philosophy have become so ascendant that they might be said to form the New Establishment of defense strategists. The New Establishment is especially strong in the Army. As a result, much of the service is being reconceptualized into a constabulary force in which nation-building and stability operations all but trump force-on-force warfighting.

Scrutinizing Past Conflicts

It is, of course, a truism that forgetting the lessons of any conflict is unwise—there is always something to learn. At the same time, allowing assumptions about the "lessons" to go unchallenged carries great potential to distort strategic thinking to the point where real vulnerabilities arise. The aim of this article is to suggest that strategists today should scrutinize the supposed "lessons" before embarking on a path that may lead the nation to the wrong destination. It cautions that the lessons of Iraq must not translate into an erosion of the Army's capability to engage in high-intensity conventional conflicts. It also argues that the manpower-intensive "Iraq-style" approach to the challenge of counterinsurgency (COIN) and irregular warfare is not necessarily the right lesson for U.S. military professionals to learn from Iraq.

That said, the New Establishment theories are correct in many respects. It is accurate, for example, to say that following the withdrawal from Vietnam, the Army focused on high-end conflict against peer-competitor states, most specifically the Soviet Union. Because of this "mistake," the critics maintain, the Army was wholly unprepared to meet the asymmetrical challenge of Iraq's insurgency in the 21st century.

Nonetheless, was the Army's post-Vietnam focus really the horrendous miscalculation so many deem it was? Even with the benefit of hindsight, the Army's strategy seems rather prescient—indeed, wise. In fact, the U.S. military was not called upon to fight another major insurgency for nearly 30 years. During that period, America's Army faced down the masses of its Soviet counterpart while at the same time successfully fighting a series of brushfire conflicts in Grenada, Panama, and elsewhere.

In the grand scheme of defense planning, "getting it right" for three decades is an exceptionally fine record. This is especially true when one considers that during this period, a genuinely existential threat to the very survival of the U.S. was not just contained, but actually driven to collapse—all without the need for a single American soldier to die in combat against that threat.

An Effective Cold War Strategy

If the U.S. had converted its Army into a constabulary/counterinsurgency force as some believe it should have, one must consider whether doing so might have invited more aggressive behavior from a declining but still militarily powerful Soviet Union.

There have been numerous instances where a nation has sought to divert attention from internal problems by engaging in external aggression. Many experts believe that Argentina, for example, precipitated the 1982 Falklands-Malvinas war for just such reasons. Furthermore, the military junta misperceived the ability of the British military, then in a period of reconfiguration, to project conventional armed force thousands of miles distant. Plainly, if there is a perception of conventional weakness, some adversaries will seek to exploit it.

The old-line Communists who were still influential in the later stages of the Soviet Union might have contemplated just such a strategy if the post-Vietnam U.S. military had converted itself into a counterinsurgency force. Other nations around the globe, North Korea among them, might have thought militarily confronting America was in the realm of the doable if the Army had been postured to fight principally low-tech, "irregular" opponents instead of one with nearly 7,000 armored vehicles and 20,000 artillery tubes. Obviously, the history of the latter part of the 20th century could have been very different had the Army embraced the supposed lessons of Vietnam in the way the New Establishment would have had it do. . . .

Blind to Other Possibilities

One of the most prominent—yet most problematic—lessons the New Establishment seems to be drawing from Iraq is that most future conflicts involving the U.S. will be some replay of Iraq (or Afghanistan). Propelling this belief are many of the Army's junior and mid-grade officers whose combat experiences in one or both countries consume their thinking to the point where they are blind to other possibilities—despite, for example, Russia's conventional assault on Georgia in summer 2008.

The depth of the New Establishment's belief is such that "Iraq-style counterinsurgency" as the Army's "organizing principle" is being seen everywhere in doctrinal documents. The tilt is hardly limited to FM 3-24 [the COIN Field Manual issued in December 2006]. One need look no further than the Army's new FM 3-0, "Operations," issued in February [2008], and FM 3-07, "Stability Operations," issued in October [2008], to find additional convincing evidence that the New Establishment's views are firmly and pervasively in place.

What these doctrinal documents show is that the New Establishment believes not just that the U.S. will conduct more Iraq-like operations, but also that they will be carried out in essentially the same manpower-intensive way. This supposed "lesson" of Iraq underpins the enormously costly expansion of ground force numbers. Former Undersecretary of Defense for Policy Ryan Henry proclaimed in 2007 that the increase of nearly 92,000 ground troops—65,000 soldiers and 27,000 Marines—was "an adaptation to this prolonged, irregular type of campaign that we can find ourselves in."

Iraq's Real Lesson

Much evidence is emerging, however, that the real lesson of Iraq is exactly opposite of what the New Establishment thinks. Specifically, the American people do not want another "Iraq-style" operation—despite the remarkable military successes of 2007 and 2008. Even James S. Corum, one of the contributors to FM 3-24, concedes as much in his new book, *Bad Strategies: How Major Powers Fail in Counterinsurgency*. Corum concludes that the experience of Iraq has so damaged support among the American people for similar operations elsewhere that they are unlikely for the future "no matter how necessary or justified they might be."

Furthermore, polls as late as October [2008] confirm Corum's views. They show that 66 percent of Americans still oppose the Iraq war, and only 38 percent believe it was right to go to war in the first place. Remarkably, this comes at a time when 53 percent believe that the war is going well. In other words, even though Americans appreciate the success in Iraq, they regret having become involved in the first place. These polls point to a profound disinclination among the public to use American troops in precisely the fashion the Army is refashioning itself to be used.

The evidence is becoming overwhelming. For example, the Pew Research Center reports that the U.S. public "has a sharply diminished appetite for U.S. efforts to deal with an array of global problems." No doubt that much of the aversion among the electorate is due to the tragic loss of American life in five years of war, a loss made all the more hurtful by the fact that as recently as March, 42 percent of Iraqis still found attacks on U.S. forces to be "acceptable."

Additionally, the financial meltdown of fall 2008 is likely another significant factor that will dampen the inclination to conduct COIN or stability operations that would require maintaining large numbers of U.S. troops in contingency areas. The public, while still strongly supportive of its service members, is becoming increasingly—and justifiably—concerned about what some pundits are claiming is a $3 trillion bill for Iraq. All this ought to make it crystal clear that there is little chance that the American public and, most importantly, its elected leadership, would commit to any large-scale deployment of U.S. forces to engage in another "Iraq-style" COIN or stability venture for the foreseeable future.

Therefore, while no one can exclude the possibility, it would not appear prudent to fashion an Army primarily prepared for such operations, especially if the only strategy offered to conduct them requires deploying tens of thousands of American ground troops. To be clear, one may agree with Defense Secretary Robert Gates's National Defense Strategy issued in June 2008 that "[f]or the foreseeable future, winning the Long War against violent extremist movements will be the central objective of the U.S.," yet still differ with those of the New Establishment who think the lesson of Iraq for "the Long War" will be to conduct operations in anywhere near that same way the Iraq war was fought.

The Success of Small-Footprint Operations

A vital lesson of "the Long War" much overlooked by the New Establishment is that small-footprint operations can work. The relatively quiet successes in the Philippines and Colombia are more appropriate and realistic models for post-Iraq COIN operations than is Iraq. Along these lines, the 20,000-man adviser corps recommended by retired Lieutenant Colonel John Nagl and others is exactly the kind of initiative that should be adopted because it aims to keep the "face" of COIN forces to the indigenous population primarily native.

Still, too many in the New Establishment just do not want to accept the reality that masses of American ground troops—regardless of their intentions—are rarely welcome virtually anywhere in the world outside of our borders.

Yet the New Establishment stubbornly persists in the idea that hundreds of thousands of soldiers ought to be recast into urbane and cultured "stabilizers." Specifically, FM 3-24 quotes COIN expert David Galula for the proposition that the "soldier must be prepared to become . . . a social worker, a civil engineer, a schoolteacher, a nurse, a boy scout." Even if one accepts the dubious assumption that the U.S. is likely to deploy large numbers of troops for another Iraq-like operation anytime soon, the reality is that the Army does not, and cannot, and likely should not, recruit and retain masses of troops with the qualifications FM 3-24 says are required.

Perhaps some portion of the U.S. military ought to be ready to perform such "soft power" duties, but it is too much

21st-Century Technology and Skills

The Pentagon needs to make smarter uses of technology and not forget about other necessary elements and skills of 21st-century warfare—like adequate postwar planning, sufficient numbers of troops on the ground and better training in dealing with civilian populations. A skilled translator or a civil-affairs specialist could help win hearts and minds while a poorly aimed smart bomb that destroys the wrong house would lose them.

Superior technology has been America's great comparative advantage on battlefields around the world for generations. It must continue to be so.

New York Times,
"A Few Big Ideas," December 31, 2008.

to ask the bulk of the Army to acquire and maintain such a diverse set of skills in each of its soldiers. A division of labor that tasks (and funds) other elements of government with such responsibilities will better permit those in uniform to maintain unequalled excellence in the "hard power" tasks America's armed forces must always be prepared to execute.

Rethinking the Manpower-Intensive Approach

There are other lessons the New Establishment ought to rethink about the manpower-intensive approach. Consider that it is becoming increasingly evident that—contrary to the Army's recent doctrinal documents—the much-disparaged notion of killing and capturing actually is more important to COIN success than many thought. And that killing and capturing often is best done by small numbers of elite troops empowered by high technology. In evaluating Bob Woodward's new book, *The War Within: A Secret White House History 2006–2008*, the *Washington Post* insists that the surge "was not the primary factor behind the steep drop in violence there during the past 16 months." Instead, it reports that it was new covert techniques to "target and kill insurgent leaders and key individuals in extremist groups" that bred success.

Still, so powerful is the New Establishment's sense of themselves that even otherwise respected soldiers have become astonishingly deaf to the limitations of an Army focused mainly on confronting another low-tech Iraq-type foe. Recently retired Colonel Peter Mansoor, a much-admired COIN authority, claimed that the Army schooled in the streets of Baghdad also is prepared to face conventional opponents. Mansoor thinks that because combat units in Iraq "routinely use armor, artillery, mechanized infantry, attack aviation, close-air support, and other assets to accomplish their missions," the Army has not lost its capability to fight high-end conventional wars.

In war, however, the enemy gets a vote. And the enemy's ballot may include artillery, armor and—yes—airpower. The Army's COIN experience, while plainly informative on close-quarters combat that can occur anywhere on the spectrum of conflict, nevertheless hardly prepares the surface force to survive and operate under, among other things, conventional airstrikes. The Army's brand-new MRAP [mine resistant ambush protected] vehicles, for example, would be quite vulnerable to such attacks, as they would be even to the main guns of the thousands of tanks dating from the early Cold War era still in service around the world.

One can only hope that as critically important as the wars in Iraq and Afghanistan are, a lesson that emerges from these conflicts is that each must be considered in a context larger than itself. As Caspar Weinberger Jr. wrote in *Human Events* in June [2008]: "While wars of insurgency are what is happening now, it is correct to say that neither Iraq nor Afghanistan, regardless of these two wars' outcomes, will cause the downfall of America. However, a loss of any type of World War III most certainly would." Weinberger quotes [political scientist and author] George Friedman: "The United States can lose a dozen Vietnams or Iraqs and not have its (most important) interests harmed. But losing a war with a nation-state could be catastrophic."

The Next War

America needs a large and powerful Army prepared to engage innovatively across the entire spectrum of conflict as part of the joint team. Hybrid conflicts that combine elements of low- and high-intensity war will be common in the 21st century (as they were in many wars of the past). The point is that excessive focus on one sort of operation—and particularly the type that every indicator suggests that the American people are loathe to repeat—as an organizing principle puts at risk the entire armed forces' ability to provide decision makers with options that reflect the military's fullest potential.

While we have got to do what we must to win our current conflicts, that does not mean we have to fight the inevitable next war the same way, even if it is an irregular war scenario. If the "lessons of Iraq" are that America's armed forces must focus largely on preparing for more Iraq-like operations, and that it should execute them in a way that requires the extended deployment of masses of U.S. troops, then those are indeed lessons that should be forgotten. It is, however, time to learn the right lessons from Iraq through unvarnished and realistic analysis.

This means we must explore how technology might serve to limit the numbers of young Americans who must be sent in harm's way. Certainly, we should unapologetically look for opportunities to replace people with machines. In that regard we need to acquire systems that can flexibly and economically be employed across the full spectrum of conflict. We also must institutionalize more aggressively the tactics, techniques, and procedures that the relatively small numbers of U.S. advisers in the Philippines, Colombia, and elsewhere used to produce progress in COIN efforts.

Recalling the timeless lesson President [Dwight D.] Eisenhower's words evoke could illuminate our thinking: "Every war is going to astonish you in the way it has occurred and in the way it is carried out." Relying on the experience in just one kind of conflict to redefine America's military carries the dangerous potential to have the nation learn the harsh lessons of defeat on tomorrow's battlefields where the enemy chooses not to fight as Iraqi insurgents did.

> "*[Private security forces] perform a valuable function. Because so many contractors are pulling guard duty ... more soldiers and marines are free for pacification operations.*"

Private Military Forces Serve an Important Function

Max Boot

Despite some bad apples, private military contractors perform a much-needed function—they free up U.S. soldiers and marines to do their jobs, maintains Max Boot in the following viewpoint. Although private military contractors are paid, they do not have the same benefits that active-duty soldiers have, he asserts. Nevertheless, Boot argues, most heroically put their lives on the line to help America's war effort. Rather than demonize private military forces, the military should enforce laws that increase their accountability and better oversee contracted operations, he reasons. Boot is a national security scholar at the Council on Foreign Relations.

As you read, consider the following questions:

1. According to Boot, why do different people dislike the private military industry?

Max Boot, "Accept the Blackwater Mercenaries," *Los Angeles Times*, October 3, 2007. Reproduced by permission of the author.

2. Why is the problem of being overly aggressive worse among private contractors, in the author's view?

3. How does the author believe mix-ups such as the one that occurred in Fallujah in 2004 can be avoided?

Like a volcano finally erupting after repeated rumblings, the actions of a Blackwater USA team in Baghdad last month [September 2007] have brought to the surface a scalding gusher of animosity toward the private military industry. Everyone, it seems, has a reason to hate the men in black.

American soldiers dislike them because they get paid a lot more for similar work. Iraqis dislike them because they have become a symbol of infringements on their sovereignty. And many American leftists dislike them because they are seen as war profiteers.

Assuming the Worst

Given all this antipathy, it is easy to assume the worst about military contractors, justified or not. Take the September 16 incident, in which at least 11 Iraqis were killed and which was the impetus for a House hearing Tuesday. Blackwater says its employees fired in self-defense after being attacked. Iraqis claim that the Blackwaterites fired indiscriminately and without provocation. There is no reason to assume—as so many critics do—that the more damning version is true, especially because the harshest condemnations have come from the Iraqi Interior Ministry, a notorious hotbed of sectarianism.

Whatever the facts in this particular case . . . , there is no doubt that there have been plenty of incidents of contractors killing civilians. But then, there have also been plenty of incidents of coalition and Iraqi soldiers killing civilians. That's what happens in a war zone, especially when your enemies don't wear uniforms.

Are some contractors overly aggressive? Of course. But so are some soldiers. Admittedly, the problem is probably worse among contractors. They are not tasked with defeating the insurgency, so they do not have to take into account the feelings of the locals, as soldiers are supposed to do. All they have to do is to get their convoys or VIPs [very important persons] safely to their destinations. (. . . Blackwater founder Erik Prince said that although 30 employees have died in Iraq, the company has never lost a diplomatic protectee there.)

Some of their actions in completing their missions can set back attempts to win "hearts and minds" [of the resident population, such as building schools and hospitals instead of conquering by brute force], but they do perform a valuable function. Because so many contractors are pulling guard duty (estimates range from 20,000 to 50,000), more soldiers and marines are free for pacification operations.

The Motives of Mercenaries

Most contractors aren't outlaws or cowboys. Even Peter Singer of the Brookings Institution, a critic of the industry, concedes that "most are highly talented ex-soldiers." Though they get paid more than their active-duty counterparts, they have less job security and lack the medical, retirement, and other benefits.

Of course they're in Iraq to make money, but the vast majority wouldn't accept a paycheck from just anyone. Most are willing to put their lives on the line only because they are helping the American war effort. And in many cases, they have performed heroically.

In 2004, for instance, an eight-man Blackwater team held off Muqtada al-Sadr's gunmen, who were besieging a Coalition Provisional Authority office in Najaf. A Marine who fought alongside the Blackwater team (and was evacuated for medical treatment by a Blackwater helicopter) received a Silver Star; if the contractors had been wearing U.S. uniforms, they undoubtedly would have received decorations too.

An Experienced Combat Force

Many, if not most, security contractors are former soldiers, often with considerable combat experience; they are generally considered more effective at their jobs than new Army recruits. Young soldiers fresh out of training often suffer from the "22-year-old syndrome," panicking and firing their weapons in no particular direction when they come under fire, says an industry insider who requested he not be identified. "This tends to be damaging to local populations, buildings, that sort of thing."

On the other hand, [Doug] Brooks says contractors, many of whom have as much as 20 years' experience in the field, tend to keep their cool under fire. "Combat is combat, of course, but security contractors tend to be far more professional," he says. "When you hire somebody with that kind of experience, you're getting quite a product."

Mary Cooper, "Privatizing the Military,"
CQ Researcher, June 25, 2004.

The problem is that a few wrongdoers spoil the reputation of the rest. There have been far too many instances of companies submitting fraudulent bills, not doing what they promised, or hiring unqualified thugs.

Addressing Problems

The answer isn't to demonize the entire private military industry, at least not unless we want to recruit so many more soldiers that we no longer have to rely on contractors. It would take about 200,000 *more* soldiers to return the Army to its early 1990s size, when there was much less reliance on contractors.

Assuming that we will be stuck with the mercenaries for the foreseeable future, we need better safeguards to limit their abuses and to integrate them better with the military.

It is outrageous that almost no American contractors have been held criminally liable for conduct in Iraq or Afghanistan, but hundreds of soldiers have been court-martialed. You can't blame this shortcoming on the security firms; they don't have the power to send their own employees to jail.

The problem is that there is a gray zone in the law when it comes to contractors on foreign battlefields. Congress has passed legislation to make clear that contractors fall within the Uniform Code of Military Justice as well as civilian law (the Military Extraterritorial Jurisdiction Act), but neither the Department of Justice nor the Judge Advocate General's Corps has shown much enthusiasm for enforcing these rules. That needs to change.

Integrating Private Contractors

Beyond that, we need to do a better job of integrating contractors with military units so as to avoid mix-ups such as the one that occurred in 2004 when four Blackwater employees were killed in Fallujah, triggering a Marine offensive. Malcolm Nance, a veteran intelligence operative who has worked as a contractor in Iraq, makes an intriguing suggestion in the *Small Wars Journal*: Create a "force protection command" within the U.S. military that would be responsible for overseeing contractor operations. This would help make contractors more useful to military commanders.

Under the right circumstances, we could even expand the use of private companies. In the past, I have suggested hiring private firms to end the genocide in Darfur.

Such proposals may seem outlandish at first blush, but only because of the negative reputation, only partly deserved, that mercenaries have acquired over the centuries. If we can figure out how to limit their abuses and hold them accountable for their conduct, it makes sense to continue using "free lances" (as mercenaries were styled in Renaissance Italy) to supplement the efforts of our overstretched armed forces.

> *"The responsibility of the State to protect human rights does not stop with contracting or subcontracting."*

Private Military Forces Must Be Made Publicly Accountable to Protect Human Rights

United Nations High Commissioner for Human Rights

The following viewpoint relates the findings of a United Nations (UN) Working Group on the use of private military and security companies (PMSCs) in Iraq and Afghanistan. While acknowledging that the U.S. Congress has taken some steps toward improving the regulation, transparency, and accountability of such private military forces, the Working Group asserts that further progress must be made to ensure that human rights are not being violated by PMSCs. The Working Group offers a number of recommendations for the U.S. government, such as enabling victims of human rights abuses at the hands of PMSCs to have access to justice and the regular release of statistics on the number of contractors injured or killed in support of U.S. military opera-

"Press Statement: UN human rights experts encouraged by US Government efforts to increase oversight and accountability over private security contractors but concerned by gaps in access to effective remedy for victims of human rights violations," United Nations High Commissioner for Human Rights, August 3, 2009. Reprinted with the permission of the United Nations.

tions. The UN Office of the High Commissioner for Human Rights oversees global programs in protecting human rights and implementing international rights agreements.

As you read, consider the following questions:

1. What is one example of an abuse by contractors in Iraq and Afghanistan the UN Working Group gives?

2. According to the Working Group, how many criminal offenses and human rights violations were formally launched by the U.S. Justice Department as of August 3, 2009?

3. What specific information does the Working Group recommend the U.S. government make available to the public?

The UN [United Nations] Working Group on the use of mercenaries concluded its official two-weeks' visit to the United States of America on 3 August 2009. . . .

The Working Group [WG] has been increasingly focusing on the impact of the activities of PMSCs [private military and security companies] on the enjoyment of human rights. Violations of human rights committed by private security contractors may include excessive use of force which could lead to injuries or death and which, prior to January 2009, were often not adequately investigated and prosecuted by the relevant authorities. The Working Group received reports of abuses by PMSCs in Iraq and Afghanistan, including the use of contractors for the interrogation of detainees in US custody. The Working Group also collected worrying information on the possible use of a private military and security company in rendition flights [a term referring to the transportation of detainees from one country to another for imprisonment without due process].

Congress Has Taken Some Positive Steps

In the last few years and especially following the Nisour Square massacre of 16 September 2007 in Baghdad [during which guards working for the private firm Blackwater killed 17 Iraqi civilians], the US Congress repeatedly expressed its concern at the lack of proper regulations for the oversight of PMSCs. The Working Group is pleased that the US Government has since taken serious corrective actions and welcomes recent adoption by the US authorities of legislations and regulations aimed at strengthening further the oversight and accountability of PMSCs such as Section 862 of the National Defense Authorization Act [for Fiscal Year 2008] (28 January 2008) and the Department of Defense "Interim Final Rule" (17 July 2009).

Moreover, the Working Group is encouraged by recent initiatives of the Congress to adopt legislation to further improve the transparency, accountability, information sharing and coordination among the contractors and the military. The Congress should pursue its efforts to adopt legislation that comprehensively provides criminal jurisdiction over contractors and civilian employees.

Transparency and Accountability Mechanisms Must Be Implemented to Protect Human Rights

Although the US authorities have put in place mechanisms to better monitor PMSCs, there is still very little information accessible to the public on the scope and type of contracts. The lack of transparency is particularly significant when companies subcontract to others. The Working Group would like to reiterate that the responsibility of the State to protect human rights does not stop with contracting or subcontracting. It is indeed the responsibility of the State to ensure that any contractor to which it outsources its functions fully respects human rights and, in cases of violations, is prosecuted and held accountable.

The Working Group is greatly concerned that PMSCs contracted by US intelligence agencies are not subject to public scrutiny due to classified information. The Working Group believes the public should have the right to access information on the scope, type and value of those contracts. The Working Group hopes that the US Government will take the necessary steps to remove all obstacles to transparency and accountability on the intelligence activities contracted to PMSCs in order to ensure full respect for and protection of human rights and prevent any situation that may lead to impunity of contractors for violations of human rights.

The Department of Justice has a key role to play to ensure application of the stated commitment of the US Government that criminal offenses and violations of human rights will not remain unpunished, and the fulfillment of the US Government's legal obligations under several international human rights treaties. To date, 17 cases involving a range of contractors in several countries and a broad range of crimes were formally launched by the Justice Department. The Working Group was informed that at least 7 convictions were pronounced. The Working Group calls on US prosecutors to play a more proactive role in investigating and prosecuting allegations of human rights violations.

Some US Policies Are Cause for Concern

The Working Group is concerned by the stated US policy intention to increase the number of private security contractors to match the surge in troops in Afghanistan. "We are particularly preoccupied that the use of PMSCs to protect US forward operating bases in most places in Afghanistan may further dilute the distinction between military and civilian personnel, an obligation under international humanitarian law. We are also alarmed by the trend towards an extensive privatization of the war. The Working Group received assurances from the US Government that it is not and does not intend to relinquish its State monopoly of the legitimate use of force", said [Working Group Chairperson-Rapporteur Shaista] Shameem.

The Working Group is also concerned by the recent objection expressed by the [Barack Obama] administration to a prohibition in the 2010 defense funding bill of the use of contractor personnel from interrogating persons detained during or in the aftermath of hostilities. "In light of the alleged involvement of PMSCs in the ill-treatment of detainees in US custody, the Working Group calls on the US Government to reconsider its initial position."

Finally, the WG believes that in addition to national regulation, an international instrument establishing an international oversight and monitoring mechanism is necessary and calls upon the US authorities to engage constructively in the international process towards the elaboration of a possible new international convention to achieve an international framework regulating the use of private contractors for security functions. In this regard, the Working Group was informed that a number of members of Congress introduced a draft bill which "directs the Secretary of State to work on existing or new international fora to achieve an international framework regulating the use of private contractors for security functions".

Preliminary Recommendations

• Congress should adopt legislation that comprehensively provides criminal jurisdiction over contractors and civilian employees, including those working for the intelligence agencies and ensure its effective implementation;

• The Department of Justice (DOJ) should ensure prompt and effective investigation of any allegations of human rights violations committed by PMSCs and prosecute alleged perpetrators. For that purpose, the DOJ should strengthen its investigative resource capacity and appoint an independent prosecutor;

• When contracting and sub-contracting, the US Government should ensure victims' right to an effective remedy and ensure that victims have access to justice; the right to remedy should also include access to a fair administrative process to claim compensations;

• DOJ should promptly make public statistical information on the status of these cases, disaggregated by the type, year, and country of alleged offence; investigations launched; prosecutions; and penalties;

• The US Government and Congress should press for further transparency and freedom of information and reduce the application of classified information as well as State secret privileges in court, in particular regarding alleged human rights violations involving PMSCs;

• The US Government should make available to the public specific information on the number of PMSCs operating under US contracts, the names of the companies, the number of personnel, weapons and vehicles as well as the activities for which they were contracted, within legitimate limitations such as national security and privacy;

• The US Government should regularly release statistics on the number of private military and security contractors injured or killed while supporting US operations;

• The US Government should consider establishing a specific system of federal licensing of PMSCs and especially of their contracts for operations abroad. Such licensing should include obligatory training of personnel on norms of international humanitarian and human rights law, and require the verified absence of national and international criminal record among PMSCs' employees;

• The US Government should put in place a vetting procedure before awarding contracts. This would require an assessment of past performance, including steps taken to provide remedy, compensation to victims for past abuses and prevent further abuses. Otherwise, suspended or convicted companies and employees involved in human rights abuses should be banned;

• Congress should launch an investigation on the use of PMSCs on rendition flights.

| "The entire system of military procurement is pervaded by dishonesty."

Procurement for the Armed Forces Is Corrupt

Robert Higgs

In capitalist countries, the government procurement of military goods from private business corrupts both parties, argues Robert Higgs in the following viewpoint. While some defense contractors and procurement decision makers are caught giving and receiving bribes, even more are not caught, he claims. In fact, the armed forces themselves support this corruption by mounting defense budgets, Higgs maintains. Thus, he reasons, to continue the flow of this ill-gotten gain, defense contractors, procurement officials, and the armed forces extort ever-increasing amounts of money from American taxpayers. Higgs, a political economy scholar at The Independent Institute, is editor of the Independent Review.

As you read, consider the following questions:

1. According to Higgs, how does the line become blurred with military-economic fascism?

Robert Higgs, "Military Economic Fascism: How Business Corrupts Government, and Vice Versa," *The Independent Review*, vol. 12, Fall 2007, pp. 299–303, 305–311. Copyright © 2007 by the Independent Institute. Reproduced by permission of *The Independent Institute*, 100 Swan Way, Oakland, CA 94021-1428 USA. http://www.independent.org/publications/article.asp?id=1896.

2. What falls under the category of legal theft, in the author's opinion?

3. What does the author argue changed in 1940?

In countries such as the United States, whose economies are commonly, though inaccurately, described as "capitalist" or "free market," war and preparation for war systematically corrupt both parties in the state-private transactions by which the government obtains the bulk of its military goods and services. On one side, business interests seek to bend the state's decisions in their favor by corrupting official decision makers with outright and de facto bribes. The outright bribes include cash, gifts in kind, loans, entertainment, transportation, lodging, prostitutes' services, inside information about personal investment opportunities, overly generous speaking fees, and promises of future employment or consulting patronage for officials or their family members. The de facto bribes include campaign contributions (sometimes legal, sometimes illegal), sponsorship of political fund-raising events, and donations to charities or other causes favored by the relevant government officials. Reports of this sort of corruption appear from time to time in the press under the rubric of "military scandal." On the other, much more important side, the state corrupts businesspeople by effectively turning them into coconspirators in and beneficiaries of its most fundamental activity—plundering the general public.

Participants in the military-industrial-congressional complex (MICC) are routinely blamed for mismanagement; frequently accused of waste, fraud, and abuse; and from time to time indicted for criminal offenses. All of these unsavory actions, however, are typically viewed as "aberrations"—misfeasances to be rectified or malfeasances to be punished while retaining the basic system of state-private cooperation in the production of military goods and services. I maintain, in contrast, that these offenses and even more serious ones are not simply unfortunate blemishes on a basically sound arrangement, but surface expressions of a thoroughgoing, intrinsic rottenness in the entire setup.

The Weight of Military-Economic Fascism

It is regrettable in any event for people to suffer under the weight of a state and its military apparatus, but the present arrangement—a system of military-economic fascism as instantiated in the United States by the MICC—is worse than full-fledged military-economic socialism. In the latter, people are oppressed by being taxed, conscripted, and regimented, but they are not co-opted and corrupted by joining forces with their rapacious rulers; a clear line separates them from the predators on the "dark side." In the former, however, the line becomes blurred, and a substantial number of people actively hop back and forth across it: Advisory committees, such as the Defense Science Board and the Defense Policy Board, and university administrators meet regularly with Pentagon officials. The revolving door spins furiously: According to a September 2002 report [by Michelle Ciarrocca in *Foreign Policy in Focus*], "[t]hirty-two major [George W.] Bush appointees are former executives, consultants, or major shareholders of top weapons contractors," and a much greater number cross the line at lower levels.

Moreover, military-economic fascism, by empowering and enriching wealthy, intelligent, and influential members of the public, removes them from the ranks of potential opponents and resisters of the state and thereby helps to perpetuate the state's existence and its intrinsic exploitation of people outside the precinct of the state and its major supporters. Thus, it simultaneously strengthens the state and weakens civil society, even as it creates the illusion of a vibrant private sector patriotically engaged in supplying goods and services to the heroic military establishment (the Boeing Company's slickly produced television ads, among others, splendidly illustrate this propagandistically encouraged illusion).

The Corruption of Government Officials

We need not dwell long on the logic of garden-variety military-economic corruption. As pots of honey attract flies, so pots of money attract thieves and con artists. No organization has more money at its disposal than the U.S. government, which attracts thieves and con artists at least in full proportion to its control of wealth. Unscrupulous private parties who desire to gain a slice of the government's booty converge on the morally dismal swamp known as Washington, D.C., and take whatever actions are necessary to divert a portion of the loot into their own hands. Anyone who expects honor among thieves will be sorely disappointed by the details of these sordid activities.

Although headlines alone cannot convey the resplendently lurid details, they can suggest the sorts of putrid sloughs that drain into the swamp:

- Audit Cites Pentagon Contractors [for widespread abuse of overhead charges]

- Ex-Unisys Official Admits Paying Bribes to Get Pentagon Contracts

- Top Republican on a House Panel Is Charged with Accepting Bribes

- Washington: Ex-Pentagon Officials Sentenced [for taking monetary bribes and accepting prostitutes' services paid for by contractors]. . .

Anyone who cares to accumulate all such news articles may look forward to full employment for the rest of his life.

Notwithstanding the many culprits who are caught in the act, one must realistically assume that a far greater number get away scot-free. As Ernest Fitzgerald, an extraordinarily knowledgeable authority with almost fifty years of relevant personal experience, has observed, the entire system of military procurement is pervaded by dishonesty: "Government officials, from the majestic office of the president to the lowest, sleaziest procurement office, lie routinely and with impunity in defense of the system," and "the combination of loose procurement rules and government acquiescence in rip-offs leaves many a crook untouched." . . .

The truly big bucks, of course, need not be compromised in the least by this sweaty species of fraud and workaday corruption. Just as someone who kills one person is a murderer, whereas someone who kills a million persons is a statesman, so the government officials who steer hundreds of billions of dollars, perhaps without violating any law or regulation, to the "star wars" contractors and the producers of other big-ticket weapon systems account for the bulk of the swag laundered through the Department of Defense and the Department of Homeland Security. I am not saying that this huge component of the MICC, although operating lawfully, is squeaky clean— far from it—but that the corruption in this area, in dollar terms, falls mainly under the heading of legal theft, or at least in the gray area. As a Lockheed employee once wrote to Fitzgerald, "The government doesn't really need this stuff. It's just the best way to get rich quick. If they really needed all these nuclear bombs and killer satellites, they wouldn't run this place the way they do." I personally recall Fitzgerald's saying to me twenty years ago at Lafayette College, "A defense contract is just a license to steal." . . .

How Government Corrupts Business

A brief review of the history of U.S. military contracting helps to clarify my claim that military-economic transactions tend to corrupt business. The most important historical fact is that before 1940, except during wartime, such dealings amounted to very little. The United States had only a tiny standing army and no standing munitions industry worthy of the name. When wars occurred, the government supplemented the products of its own arsenals and navy yards with goods and services purchased from private contractors, but most such items were off-the-shelf civilian goods, such as boots, clothing, food, and transportation services. To be sure, plenty of occasions arose for garden-variety corruption in these dealings—bribes, kickbacks, provision of shoddy goods, and so forth—but such malfeasances were usually one-shot or fleeting transgressions because the demobilization that followed the conclusion of each war removed the opportunity for such corruption to become institutionalized to a significant degree in law, persistent organizations, or ongoing practice. Like gaudy fireworks, these sporadic outbursts of corruption flared brightly and then turned to dead cinders. No substantial peacetime contracting existed to fuel enduring corruption of the military's private suppliers, and much of the contracting that did take place occurred within the constraints of rigid solicitations and sealed-bid offers, which made cozy deals between a military buyer and a private seller difficult to arrange. As late as fiscal year 1940, the War Department made 87 percent of its purchases through advertising and invitations to bid.

These conditions changed abruptly and forever in 1940: The challenges that the government faced during the two years before the United States became a declared belligerent in World War II and the manner in which it responded to them had an enduring effect in shaping the contours of the MICC and hence in establishing its characteristic corruption of business.

The [Franklin Delano] Roosevelt administration, desperate to build up the nation's capacity for war after the breathtaking German triumphs in the spring of 1940, made an abrupt about-face, abandoning its relentless flagellation of businessmen and investors and instead courting their favor as prime movers in the buildup of the munitions industries. Most of

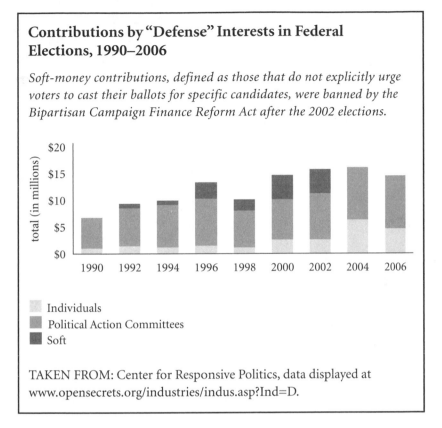

Contributions by "Defense" Interests in Federal Elections, 1990–2006

Soft-money contributions, defined as those that do not explicitly urge voters to cast their ballots for specific candidates, were banned by the Bipartisan Campaign Finance Reform Act after the 2002 elections.

Individuals
Political Action Committees
Soft

TAKEN FROM: Center for Responsive Politics, data displayed at www.opensecrets.org/industries/indus.asp?Ind=D.

the relevant businessmen, however, having been anathematized and legislatively pummeled for the previous six years, were reluctant to enter into such deals for a variety of reasons, chief among them being their fear and distrust of the federal government.

Changes in Procurement Laws

To placate the leery businessmen by shifting the risks from them onto the taxpayers, the government adopted several important changes in its procurement laws and regulations. These changes included negotiated cost-plus-fixed-fee contracts, instead of contracts arrived at within the solicitation-and-sealed-bid system; various forms of tax breaks; government loan guarantees; direct government funding of plants, equipment, and raw materials; and provision of advance and progress payments, sparing the contractors the need to obtain and pay interest on bank loans. All of these arrangements, with greater or lesser variations in their details from time to time, became permanent features of the MICC.

Even more important, as the new system operated on a vast scale during World War II, dealings between military purchasers and private suppliers assumed a fundamentally new form. . . .

Under the pre-1940 system, a private business rarely had anything to gain by wining and dining military buyers or congressmen. Unless a firm made the lowest-priced, sealed-bid offer to supply a carefully specified good, it would not get the contract. Military buyers knew what they needed, and they had a tightly limited budget with which to get it. After 1940, however, the newly established "intimate relationship" opened up a whole new world for wheeling and dealing on both sides—it was often difficult to say whether the government official was shaking down the businessman or the businessman was bribing the government official. In fact, until the military purchasing agency certified a company as qualified, the firm could not make a valid offer, even in the context of competitive bidding. In the post-1940 era, however, only a small fraction of all contracts emerged from formally advertised, sealed-bid competition, and most contracts were negotiated without any kind of price competition. . . .

Deals came to turn not on price, but on technical and scientific capabilities, size, experience, and established reputation as a military supplier—vaguer attributes that are easier to fudge for one's friends. From time to time, deals also turned on the perceived need to keep a big firm from going under. For example, Fen Hampson observes that in the early 1970s, "The bidding [for production of the C-4 (Trident I) missile] was not opened to other companies because Lockheed was encountering financial difficulties at the time and desperately needed the business."

Increasing Money for Defense

To keep this gravy train on the track, contractors and their trade associations, as well as the armed forces themselves, devote great efforts to increasing the amount of money Congress appropriates for "defense" and now also for "homeland security." Campaign contributions and other favors go predominantly to the incumbent barons—congressional leaders and committee chairmen—and to the military "hawks" who have never met a defense budget big enough to satisfy them. As Fitzgerald notes, "In Washington you can get away with anything as long as you have the high moguls of Congress as accessories before and after the fact." . . .

To give the public a seeming interest in the whole wretched racket and thus to dull their awareness of being victimized, the contractors also spend substantial amounts of money cultivating the public's yearning to have the military dish out death and destruction to designated human quarry around the world—commies, gooks, ragheads, Islamo-fascists, narco-terrorists, and so forth—who are said to threaten the precious American way of life. For example, Rockwell, a military contractor whose massive secret contributions helped to reelect Richard Nixon in 1972, once mounted "a secret grassroots campaign code-named Operation Common Sense" that included "a massive letter-writing campaign . . . solicitation of support from national organizations . . . and production of films and advertisements as well as prepared articles, columns, and editorials that willing editors could print in newspapers and magazines," [says Nick Kotz in his 1988 book *Wild Blue Yonder: Money, Politics, and the B-1 Bomber*]—all the news that's fit to print, so to speak. Much money goes into producing glorification of the armed forces—"the few, the proud, the marines," blah, blah, blah—and reports of those forces' stupidities and brutalities in exotic climes are dismissed as nothing but the fabrications of leftists and appeasers, or, if they cannot plausibly be denied, are alleged to be nothing more than the isolated misbehavior of a few "bad apples." ...

In sum, the military-supply firms exemplify a fundamentally corrupt type of organization. Their income comes to them only after it has first been extorted from taxpayers at gunpoint; hence, their compensation amounts to receiving stolen property. They are hardly unwitting or unwilling recipients of this ill-gotten booty, however, because they are not drafted to do what they do. No wallflowers at this dance of death, they eagerly devote strenuous efforts to encouraging government officials to wring ever greater amounts from the taxpayers and to distribute the loot in ways that enrich the contractors, their suppliers, and their employees. These efforts include both the licit and the illicit measures I have described, spanning the full range from making a legal campaign contribution to providing prostitutes to service the congressman or the Pentagon bigwig after he has become bored with playing poker in the contractor's suite at a plush D.C. hotel.

| "A courageous set of reforms in our defense budget ... will target waste and strengthen our military for the future."

Weapon Systems Acquisition Reforms Will Reduce Waste

Barack Obama

The Weapon Systems Acquisition Reform Act will eliminate some of the waste in U.S. defense projects, asserts U.S. president Barack Obama in the following viewpoint. Reducing waste will not only save taxpayers money, but also free up money to better protect our nation and support our troops, he claims. A lack of oversight and no-bid weapons contracts have led to inexcusable waste and, unconscionably, at a time of war, has not made our nation any safer, Obama explains. The Weapon Systems Acquisition Reform Act is a first step toward promoting accountability and regaining the public trust, he reasons.

As you read, consider the following questions:

1. What does Obama promise the American people as commander in chief?

2. According to the author, what is the purpose of the Weapon Systems Acquisition Reform Act?

Barack Obama, "Remarks by the President at Signing of the Weapons Systems Acquisition Reform Act," May 22, 2009. www.whitehouse.gov.

3. In the author's view, what do all members of Congress who worked on the act understand?

Long before I took office, I argued that meeting our greatest challenges would require not only changing policies in Washington, but changing the way we do business in Washington. It would require reforming a culture where the influence of lobbyists too often trumps the will of the people, rethinking government so that it works as effectively and efficiently as possible, and renewing our sense of common purpose so that we can bring people together in common effort.

That's exactly what we've done this week. On Tuesday [May 11, 2009], we brought auto executives, labor unions, environmental groups, Democrats, and Republicans together to set a national fuel-efficiency standard for our cars and trucks for the first time in history. On Wednesday, I signed bipartisan legislation to help homeowners and to crack down on the predatory lenders who seek to take advantage of them. And later this afternoon, I'll sign bipartisan legislation that protects consumers from the unfair rate hikes and abusive fees levied by many credit card companies.

Eliminating Waste

And this morning, I'm proud to join Democratic and Republican members of Congress for the signing of a bill that will eliminate some of the waste and inefficiency in our defense projects—reforms that will better protect our nation, better protect our troops, and save taxpayers tens of billions of dollars.

Now, let me be clear: As Commander in Chief, I will do whatever it takes to defend the American people, which is why I've increased funding for the best military in the history of the world. We'll continue to make new investments in 21st-century capabilities to meet new challenges. And we will al-

A Unanimously Supported Act

The following are the remarks of House Armed Services Committee Chairman Ike Skelton during debate on the Senate conference report to the Weapon Systems Acquisition Reform Act of 2009; the House unanimously agreed, and the President signed the bill the next day.

Congress will speak with a single voice and will at the same time adopt tough medicine for the [weapons] acquisition system. . . . The consensus on this legislation is simply the result of a problem that has become so obvious, and so urgent, that every member has concluded that strong action is required.

Too often under our current acquisition system, we end up with too few weapons that cost us too much and arrive too late. [The Government Accountability Office] tells us that [Department of Defense] will exceed its original cost estimates on 96 major weapon systems by $296 billion. That is more than two years of pay and health care for all of our troops. We can no longer tolerate this state of affairs. . . . The status quo of indiscipline and inefficiency in acquisition is no longer an option.

Ike Skelton,
Remarks Delivered During the House Debate on
the Conference Report to S. 454, the Weapon Systems
Acquisition Reform Act of 2009, May 21, 2009.

ways give our men and women in uniform the equipment and the support that they need to get the job done.

But I reject the notion that we have to waste billions of taxpayer dollars to keep this nation secure. When it comes to purchasing weapons systems and developing defense projects, the choice we face is between investments that are designed to keep the American people safe and those that are simply designed to make a defense company or a contractor rich.

Last year, the Government Accountability Office, or the GAO, looked into 95 major defense projects and found cost overruns that totaled $295 billion. Wasteful spending comes from exotic requirements, lack of oversight, and indefensible no-bid contracts that don't make our troops or our country any safer. To put this in perspective, these cost overruns would have paid our troops' salaries and provided benefits for their families for more than a year.

At a time when we're fighting two wars and facing a serious deficit, this is inexcusable and unconscionable. As Secretary [of Defense Robert M.] Gates has said, one dollar of waste in our defense budget is a dollar we can't spend to support our troops, or prepare for future threats, or protect the American people. Well, it's finally time to end this waste and inefficiency.

Already I've announced reform that will greatly reduce no-bid defense contracts and save the government billions of dollars. And Secretary Gates, working with our military leadership, has also proposed a courageous set of reforms in our defense budget that will target waste and strengthen our military for the future. In taking on this enormously difficult task, he's done a tremendous job, and I want to publicly commend Secretary Gates for that.

The Weapon Systems Acquisition Reform Act

The bill I'm signing today, known as the Weapon Systems Acquisition Reform Act, represents an important next step in this procurement reform process. It reforms a system where taxpayers are charged too much for weapons systems that too often arrive late—a system that suffers from spending on unproven technologies, outdated weapons, and a general lack of oversight.

The purpose of this law will be to limit cost overruns before they spiral out of control. It will strengthen oversight and accountability by appointing officials who will be charged with closely monitoring the weapons systems we're purchasing to ensure that costs are controlled. If the cost of certain defense projects continues to grow year after year, those projects will be closely reviewed, and if they don't provide the value we need, they will be terminated. This law will also enhance competition and end conflicts of interest in the weapons acquisitions process so that American taxpayers and the American military can get the best weapons at the lowest cost.

And this legislation is long overdue, and it's been a long time coming. But we're finally signing it into law because of the dedication and commitment of a few key members of Congress who've been fighting for years for this reform: Senators Carl Levin and John McCain; Representatives Ike Skelton, John McHugh, Rob Andrews, and Mike Conaway. I'm very proud of the extraordinary work that all these gentlemen have done who are standing behind me today. Senator McCain couldn't be here today because he's making sure he has a good seat to watch his son graduate from the [United States] Naval Academy in a few hours, and that's where I'm headed as soon as I catch my ride over here.

Unanimous Support

But I will tell you that defense procurement reform was one of the issues that John McCain and I discussed in our first meeting after the election. We pledged to work together to get it done, and today I'm extraordinarily proud to stand here and sign a bill that passed with unanimous support from both parties at every step of the way.

What all the gentlemen standing behind me, as well as Senator McCain, know, what Secretary Gates knows, what all members of Congress who have worked on this legislation understand, is that we have no greater responsibility than to ensure that our men and women in uniform have everything they need to do their jobs. And every penny we waste on this effort because of no-bid contracts or cost overruns is not only an affront to American taxpayers, it's an affront to our military. And while we have a long way to go to end this waste once and for all, the legislation I'm about to sign is a very important step in creating a government that is more efficient, more accountable, and more responsible in keeping the public's trust.

Periodical Bibliography

The following articles have been selected to supplement the diverse views presented in this chapter.

Robert Burton and Jerry Cox	"Reforming Defense Procurement; No 'Fiscal Responsibility' Without Tackling Military Expenditures," *Washington Times*, February 25, 2009.
Mary H. Cooper	"Privatizing the Military," *CQ Researcher*, June 25, 2004.
Charles J. Dunlap Jr.	"We Still Need the Big Guns," *New York Times*, January 9, 2008.
Peter Grier	"Record Number of US Contractors in Iraq," *Christian Science Monitor*, August 18, 2008.
Heike Hasenauer	"Defending America . . . from Space," *Soldiers Magazine*, April 2009.
Dave Hickey	"Companies Must Set and Review Compliance Priorities," *National Defense*, January 2007.
Richard H. Kohn	"Tarnished Brass: Is the U.S. Military Profession in Decline?" *World Affairs*, Spring 2009.
New York Times	"A Few Big Ideas," December 31, 2008.
Joshua S. Press	"Crying Havoc over the Outsourcing of Soldiers and Democracy's Slipping Grip on the Dogs of War," *Northwestern University Law Review Colloquy*, 2008.
John Sayen	"Next Shoe: As Economy Sinks, Will Military Follow?" *Defense News*, January 26, 2009.
Rafael Enrique Valero	"Hired Guns," *National Journal*, January 5, 2008.

What Policies Best Govern Armed Forces Personnel?

Chapter Preface

One of several controversies in the debate over what policies best govern armed forces personnel is the military's policy of involuntary enlistment extensions, also known as its stop-loss policy. When men and women sign up for service, they typically do so for a set period. To maintain troop levels in the war on terror, however, the U.S. Army has ordered both active-duty personnel and Army reservists and National Guard members to stay with their units for the duration of the unit's deployment, even if their contracts have been completed. These stop-loss periods can reach two years or even longer. While some claim this stop-loss policy is, essentially, a draft and a fraudulent way to maintain troop levels, others say the policy is legal and necessary to maintain troop unity.

Supporters argue that the policy is not designed to compensate for personnel shortages but to keep units that have trained and work well together intact. According to Army spokesperson Bryan Hilferty, quoted in Pamela M. Prah's 2005 article in *CQ Researcher*, "The nation is at war, and we are 'stop-lossing' units deploying to a combat theater to ensure they train, deploy, fight and redeploy as a team." The Army, he reasons, learned this lesson from the Vietnam War. "We don't want to do Vietnam," Hilferty argues, in a 2006 *Tampa Tribune* article, "where a guy comes into the platoon in the middle of the fight to replace a guy who just left." Claims that the armed forces are fraudulently inducing people to serve longer tours are misinformed, policy proponents contend. Enlistees voluntarily agree to these terms when they sign up, supporters maintain, and they are informed that the terms of the agreement are not promises and that Congress may change or add to their obligations.

Critics dispute this claim, maintaining that stop-loss policies essentially break the contracts the Army has made with service members and violates the concept of a volunteer army. Andrew Exum, a former army captain, called the policy disgraceful in a June 2004 *New York Times* article. He reasons that "many, if not most, of the soldiers in this latest Iraq-bound wave are already veterans of several tours in Iraq and Afghanistan. They have honorably completed their active-duty obligations. But like draftees, they have been conscripted to meet the additional needs in Iraq." Some National Guard members challenged their extensions in the federal courts. David W. Qualls enlisted in the National Guard's "Try-One" enlistment option that allows those with prior military experience to sign up for one year. Qualls was sent to Iraq eight months after he signed and was not allowed to come home when his term was up. Attorney Jules Lobel argues that such a tactic is, in fact, fraud.

The federal appeals court ruled otherwise, however, holding that the Defense Department does in fact have the right to require National Guard members to remain in service. Nevertheless, on March 18, 2008, Defense Secretary Robert Gates announced that the Pentagon would no longer use the controversial stop-loss policy. Despite the Pentagon's assurances, stop-loss policies remain controversial. The continuing war on terror has critics suggesting that it is premature to assume that stop-loss is a thing of the past. The authors in the following chapter explore other controversies in the debate over what policies best govern armed forces personnel.

"Experts and commanders say 15-month tours are too long because they compound mental health problems and other issues at home."

Long Tours of Duty and Repeated Deployments Should Be Reduced

Gordon Lubold

Long tours and repeated deployments have led to increasing rates of suicide and divorce among armed forces personnel, claims Gordon Lubold in the following viewpoint. Reducing the emotional toll these policies have wrought upon U.S. armed forces is reason enough to put an end to such practices, he maintains. Treating the mental health problems that stem from extended tours is also costly, Lubold argues. Unfortunately, while military leaders recognize the price troops pay for these policies, they must respond to the demands of war, he concludes. Lubold is a staff writer for the Christian Science Monitor.

Gordon Lubold, "Soldier Rampage Hints at Stress of Repeated Deployments," *Christian Science Monitor*, May 13, 2009. Copyright © 2009 The Christian Science Publishing Society. All rights reserved. Reproduced by permission from Christian Science Monitor, (www.csmonitor.com).

As you read, consider the following questions:

1. According to Lubold, what case has focused attention on the effect that multiple, extended deployments have on soldiers?

2. According to the author's claims, how many veterans have been diagnosed with some form of post-traumatic stress disorder?

3. In the author's view, what is a significant part of the problem of getting veterans to seek treatment for post-traumatic stress disorder?

Military police on Tuesday [May 12, 2009] charged Sergeant John Russell, a soldier on a 15-month tour to Iraq—his third deployment to the country—with murder in the shooting deaths of five soldiers at an American base.

Details about Sergeant Russell are beginning to emerge. In an interview with a local television station in Sherman, Texas, Russell's father [Wilburn Russell] said his son was facing financial difficulty and feared he was about to be discharged from the Army. The case has focused further attention on the effect that multiple, extended deployments are having on soldiers.

The Impact of Long, Repeated Deployments

Fifteen-month tours and repeated deployments are increasing the rate of suicide, divorce, and psychological problems, according to Pentagon data. The shootings at Camp Liberty in Iraq speak to the need "to redouble our efforts . . . in terms of dealing with the stress," said Admiral Mike Mullen, chairman of the Joint Chiefs of Staff, in a Pentagon press conference.

Defense Secretary Robert Gates is requesting to "institutionalize and properly fund" programs to help wounded troops, including those with psychological disorders. Roughly 300,000 veterans have been diagnosed with some form of post-traumatic stress disorder.

But a main source of the problem—the repeated, extended deployments—will probably continue. President [Barack] Obama is drawing troops down in Iraq, but he is also sending more to Afghanistan, minimizing the impact that the drawdown from Iraq will have on the health of the force.

Questioning Military Mental Health Care

The US military command launched an investigation Tuesday into whether it offers adequate mental health care to its soldiers. Russell's father said his son, who joined the Army in 1994, felt alienated at the stress center.

"They didn't tell him they were there for his benefit— [that] they were there as a friend to him to find out if he had any psychological problems as a result of his third tour of duty," the father, Wilburn Russell, told the local news station.

In Baghdad, Major General David Perkins told reporters that Russell, a communications specialist assigned to the 54th Engineer Battalion from Bamberg, Germany, was sent to the mental health clinic by his superiors, presumably because of concern over his emotional state.

He said the commander had prohibited Russell from carrying a weapon, but somehow he got a weapon, entered the clinic, and opened fire.

Experts and commanders say 15-month tours are too long because they compound mental health problems and other issues at home. Secretary Gates agrees. He extended Army tours from 12 to 15 months only reluctantly, saying it was needed to help support the "surge" of troops to Iraq in 2007. He has since lifted the policy, but there remain two units in Iraq still finishing 15-month tours that won't return until this summer and fall.

A Different Approach to Manning the Conflict

The whole approach to providing manpower for this conflict differs from that of the Vietnam War, from 1964–1975. Then, a much larger active military—8.7 million troops—was bolstered by a draft that added 1.7 million more soldiers to the ranks, according to the Veterans of Foreign Wars [VFW]. More than 640,000 of the draftees served in Vietnam, constituting about one-quarter of the total U.S. force there, the VFW said.

But the draft ended in 1973, and the active military now numbers about 1.4 million, according to the Department of Defense.

In order to sustain troop levels in what has become a much more prolonged conflict than originally anticipated, the military has relied on repeated deployments. . . .

Extended tours of duty in the combat zone—some as long as 18 months—also are a departure from the past. In Vietnam, the standard tour of duty was 12 months. If a soldier was to be redeployed to the combat zone, Army policy mandated a 24-month period of recuperation or retraining between tours.

Kari Huus,
"Gut Check: Iraq War's Impact at Home,"
MSNBC.com, October 15, 2007. www.msnbc.com.

Looking at Dwell Time

Yet perhaps the more important factor in stress among soldiers is "dwell time"—the amount of time the military allows service members to stay at home. The Army's current dwell time is about 12 months, meaning 12 months at home followed by a 12-month deployment. By 2012, the service hopes to double the amount of time spent at home for every 12-month tour to a war zone.

Compounding the problem is the fact that a soldier can spend weeks or even months away from home, even during dwell time.

"There are schools they have to attend, there are boxes they have to check off, in addition to checking off the boxes with their families, too," says Kathleen Moakler, director of government relations for the National Military Family Association, an advocacy group in Washington.

Army leaders recognize the problem, but when it comes to slowing the rate of deployments, their hands are largely tied until the wartime demand for forces begins to fall.

"It is a resilient force, it is an amazing force, but I've got to tell you, it's a tired and stressed force," said Gen. Peter Chiarelli, vice chief of staff for the Army, during a Senate hearing last month.

Meanwhile, the rate of those with post-traumatic stress disorder continues to climb. One in 5 veterans from Iraq or Afghanistan—about 300,000 individuals—have some form of the condition, according to a study by the RAND Corp., a security consultancy in Arlington, Virginia. A significant part of the problem is pushing vets to overcome the stigma of seeking treatment. Only slightly more than half of those 300,000 veterans have received any kind of treatment, says RAND.

Gates's proposal to expand mental health services is a start, says Tom Tarantino, a former Army officer who now works as a legislative associate for Iraq and Afghanistan Veterans of America [IAVA]. The IAVA advocates expanding the corps of mental health professionals, creating mandatory "face to face" counseling for each returning veteran, and increasing the amount of training within the military to help soldiers recognize mental health issues among their colleagues.

With more and more veterans coming home, "this is a problem that is going to persist," says Mr. Tarantino.

| "Belief that they are making a difference
in their jobs helps mitigate the immense
strain of being a soldier today."

Despite Long Tours of Duty, U.S. Soldiers Are Meeting the Challenges of War

Anna Mulrine

Although the war in Iraq has placed tremendous demands on American armed forces, these courageous servicemen and servicewomen are meeting the challenges, claims Anna Mulrine in the following viewpoint. Many soldiers have served multiple tours of combat and have seen their deployments or commitment extended, she asserts. Nevertheless, Mulrine argues, the belief that they are making a difference helps mitigate the strain. The camaraderie among combat teams and the knowledge that they are helping another country rebuild gives support to overextended troops, she maintains. Mulrine writes on military strategy and Middle East policy for U.S. News & World Report.

As you read, consider the following questions:

1. In Mulrine's opinion, how is the U.S. military wrestling over its own narrative of the Iraq war?

2. What did Del Valle, Whitten, and Jones say made a military career attractive?

3. In the author's view, why do today's soldiers not want to see a return to the draft?

On a sunny afternoon in Baqubah, a convoy of Iraqi troops and U.S. soldiers depart the small base they share on a mission to bring blankets and heating oil to a nearby village. They drive down an empty road, passing packs of dogs and curbs scarred by weeks of steady roadside bombs. Suddenly, the team's humanitarian operation turns deadly as an explosion rips into the lead Humvee. Sgt. Chester Jones and Sgt. Maj. Eddie Del Valle help rush a critically injured young sergeant to the field hospital. Jones, a medic, cradles the soldier's injured head as he vomits, while another helps change bandages soaked through with blood.

It is twilight as troops from the 3rd Brigade Combat Team, 1st Cavalry Division, tow the blasted Humvee back to base. They cover it with a tarp, then get the news that they fear. The young soldier, Sgt. Jay Gauthreaux, has died from his wounds.

That was just over one year ago. Today, Del Valle and Jones are back home at Fort Hood, Texas, after their second Iraq deployments. Like tens of thousands of this war's veterans, they look back on their time in the country with a complex mixture of pride, frustration, satisfaction, and sadness. Del Valle recalls, for instance, the emotional task of cleaning out Gauthreaux's room the morning after the attack, packing up photos of the fallen soldier's 4-year-old son. "He's the same age as my little daughter," says Del Valle, "so you put yourself in that situation." Jones saw war's human toll every day while training Iraqi Army medics, but that didn't lessen the shock of losing his good friend. "I didn't realize it was G until I ran to the truck and pulled his body back," Jones says. "With training, you learn to try and push that stuff aside," he adds, "but it's tough."

Just as wars leave a lasting mark on soldiers, they tend to change the culture of the armies that fight them. As the fifth anniversary of the invasion of Iraq approaches, American troops are reflecting on their experiences even as they await how their mission will be judged. So, too, the institution of the military is wrestling over its own narrative for this war, assessing how well America and its commanders have used one of the most powerful tools available to any nation. The lessons it takes away from the experience of its soldiers and marines will influence how it adapts and organizes itself—and how it cares for those sent to do the nation's fighting.

What is immediately clear is that this conflict has put enormous demands on American troops. They are warriors on some days, diplomats on others, in a conflict with no clear front lines and a changing cast of adversaries. And while they are grateful that the American public has steadfastly supported them, regardless of feelings about the war itself, many soldiers report a sense of disconnection, too. America as a nation is not waging this war, many tell you—its military is.

Recent security gains in Iraq, particularly the sharp declines in combat deaths, have come as a welcome development. But there remains a heavy burden on America's fighting men and women. Commanders express grave concerns for troops shouldering wars on two fronts with no end in sight, particularly the half million who have served more than one combat tour since 2002. Soldiers in Iraq, who have seen the duration of their deployments extended as a result of an inadequate post-invasion plan, work seven days a week for 15 months straight, minus two weeks for a trip home to visit family. And they do it all, they joke, without beer (American troops today are forbidden to drink while at war). More than

60,000 troops have been subjected to controversial stop-loss measures—meaning those who have completed service commitments are forbidden to leave the military until their units return from war.

Sacrifice. The news that their yearlong tour was lengthened by three months hit the team hard, says Del Valle. "That was the worst. It's like when you're real thirsty, and you're about to reach for the bottle—and somebody pulls it far away from you." Midway through medic Jones's tour, his wife called to ask for a divorce. "I'm not mad at her, because I can't blame her," he says. "She was tired of being alone." Jones has been deployed to Iraq two of the past five years, which has left him little time to see his children, now ages 4 and 2, grow up.

The sacrifices are great, and sometimes soldiers wonder why they keep making them. On the night that Gauthreaux died, Del Valle and Capt. Christopher Whitten, the gunner that day, talked about their career choice over a game of chess at a small shop on their base as the Iraqi owner served them tea and warm bread. They express a brief moment of doubt about the extent to which what they do is really understood by most Americans. "You get in a Humvee every day because that's the job that is feeding your family. I also believe in what we're doing here," says Del Valle. "Our soldiers here are giving 100 percent for every American guy back in the States." Whitten nods, adding, "It makes you wonder, does anybody really appreciate what that guy gave up today?"

It is not an uncommon question in this combat zone. Historians will tell you that wars throughout the ages, whatever their outcome, tend to wreck armies and wear out soldiers. Troops hasten to add that the belief that they are making a difference in their jobs helps mitigate the immense strain of being a soldier today. "I would argue that you haven't seen an army like this since the demise of the Roman legion—such a small number of forces able to influence the world," says Clinton Ancker III, a retired Army colonel and director of the

Meeting the Challenges

Today's soldiers and leaders find themselves dealing with a full-spectrum threat on widely differing terrain against a resourceful enemy. They interact with noncombatants and government agencies in areas ranging from urban settings to remote mountainous regions in which both the enemy and the terrain present their own uncompromising challenges. Amidst all of this, our soldiers draw upon their own and their predecessors' experience to anticipate and deal effectively with the challenges of the environment and the enemy.

Michael Barbero,
"Meeting the Challenges of the Operational Environment,"
Infantry Magazine, *November-December 2008.*

Combined Arms Doctrine Directorate. When the 3rd Brigade Combat Team arrived in Baqubah, there was widespread corruption and heartbreaking violence against civilians. During the tour of Del Valle, Whitten, and Jones's brigade, they drove out terrorists and saw some life return to the markets, children to soccer fields. It is the sort of impact that makes a military career attractive, they say.

But the desire to make a difference can lead to even greater frustration when troops return after previous tours in Iraq to find what they consider to be little change or even backsliding during a counterinsurgency campaign in which the very definition of victory is still a lively topic of debate. That frustration can be compounded, too. Ancker argues that soldiers are under "a lot more stress" now than they were in Vietnam. "The atmosphere is more physically demanding. And in Vietnam, we were guaranteed at least a year between deployments," he says. When soldiers are injured—physically and psychologically—they are at the mercy of a deeply overburdened system that they cannot always count on to take care of them.

Camaraderie. The military has drawn lessons from past wars, notably Vietnam, reorganizing the Army into brigade combat teams in part to encourage unit cohesion and camaraderie. This has promoted the sort of psychological bonding that gives troops a sense of support in the face of the enormous demands, says Jeffrey LaFace, the division chief of the Army's Combined Arms Center.

That camaraderie is clear on forward operating bases throughout Baghdad, where troops organize flag football matches and barbecues and decompress in coffee shops and Internet cafes with fellow soldiers and marines who have become close friends over the years. "Soldiers go in as units, with the same group of guys that they have known since they were privates in Kosovo and Bosnia," says LaFace. These "adopted families," he adds, help to stem "some of the weirdness that we had coming out of Vietnam." That weirdness included soldiers who shot officers when they didn't want to do a mission and riots in U.S. military prisons overcrowded with deserters.

It is another notable legacy of the troubled Vietnam-era Army that many of today's volunteer soldiers have little desire to see the nation return to the draft. "It's the only thing that would make me get out of the Army," says Capt. Scott Hubbard, who recently returned from a tour in Iraq. The last thing you want to do, he adds, is fight next to someone who doesn't want to be next to you.

Despite the strains, the retention rate for troops in Iraq remains high, commanders point out. Their concern, though, is whether it will stay that way. "The entire Army leadership—and rightfully—we get a little nervous," says Peter Chiarelli, the military assistant to Secretary of Defense Robert Gates and until 2006 the widely admired No. 2 commander in Iraq. "All of us are extremely concerned that we could cross a line without even knowing it."

Some commanders in Iraq worry that they are flirting with those lines now as demands on soldiers show little sign of letting up. There is growing evidence that post-traumatic stress is taking a toll: The number of troops who tried to commit suicide or injure themselves increased from 350 in 2002 to 2,100 last year. So, too, can the simple fear and fatigue that accompany daily patrols. One active-duty commander recalls a unit that had gone months without a serious casualty, only to have a soldier hit by a sniper weeks before the unit was scheduled to head home. The commander was approached by an officer carrying a spreadsheet that charted out the number of times company commanders had gone out on patrol or operations over a two-week period. "I had cases where I had officers who by their job nature should be going out all the time, who'd only gone out two or three times," he says. "It was probably related directly to losing soldiers, personal fear, and the fact that you're only a month or two out from going home," he continues. "I asked them, 'Have you considered the effect this has had on your soldiers?' I remember what a leadership challenge it was, and I imagine that a lot of similar things are occurring in other battalions."

Changes, challenges. Today, troops discuss such leadership challenges at countless outposts in Iraq and at the premier centers of military learning. These chats are not always pretty. Some note, for example, that Congress has fewer military veterans than in the past and, perhaps as a result, shows too much deference to the military leaders who testify on Capitol Hill. "Congress doesn't ask the tough questions they should be asking, because they're afraid that they're going to be accused of not supporting the troops," says one captain on patrol in East Baghdad. His buddy agrees. "Debates in Congress don't hurt our feelings. That's what we're here for, freedom of speech."

There is little doubt within the military itself, particularly among more junior officers, that this freedom of speech includes a growing willingness to question the decisions of commanders leading the war. That is driven in large part by the experience they are getting in the field: In today's military, the average captain has spent more time in combat than most World War II veterans—and more than some senior officers now in the military.

Indeed, military leaders acknowledge this change. "We've got to listen to the young folks—they have lived this conflict in a different way—and make sure their lessons are incorporated into this Army," Chiarelli says. "In order to do that, you've got to be willing to accept a dialogue in which many of the things that old guys like me thought are challenged."

Those challenges include new ways of thinking about how decisions are made. The Army has recently launched its own "Red Team University" to train officers to be, in essence, the opposite of yes men. Graduates of this program are then placed in brigades to question the assumptions behind decisions in hopes of averting tactical and strategic missteps. And though many argue that soldiers' grumbling about their commanders' decision is a tradition as old as the Army itself, Richard Kohn, a war historian at the University of North Carolina, believes one thing is clear: "I think that coming out of the war, you're going to have a much more candid military."

Informed support. That candor, too, must include presenting a realistic picture of the war effort to the American public, say the students at Fort Leavenworth, Kan. Not doing so in advance of the Iraq war was a mistake, they add—one that should not be repeated. "We should now consider whether we can ever successfully go to war for an extended period of time without the informed support of the American people," writes Chiarelli in a recent article for the journal *Military Review*.

But garnering that informed consent presents a dilemma: How does a military defined by its can-do culture paint a more realistic portrait of war? It might begin, troops say, with managing expectations—of the American people and of the soldiers themselves. "We expected to come in and throw another 3-pointer and everyone stand up and cheer," says Hubbard. "There was a lot of emotion, a lot of rhetoric, all the country music songs getting everybody fired up," he adds. "I think a lot of folks screaming for war—on both sides, political, civilians, military—just don't understand what it takes."

And that remains a cause of concern for troops today. Maj. Kareem Montague, an Iraq veteran and Harvard graduate, wonders too about the war's impact on a country in which only a small slice of its citizens are serving in the military, and how it may affect the civil-military relationship. "It's not that it's unhealthy, but it's becoming more and more separate," observes Montague, now a master's student in the prestigious School of Advanced Military Studies at the Command and General Staff College in Fort Leavenworth. "If you have fewer and fewer people who have served, you have to worry about whether you can have an intelligent conversation about how the military can best serve the country."

Ask soldiers here why they signed up, and many will say for duty, an instinctive feeling they have that you cannot be a citizen without doing this. Many others say the money is a big incentive—specifically, money for an education that they couldn't otherwise afford. "I did it for college, and because I had nowhere else to go," says one Baghdad-based soldier. Another confides that he sometimes feels like a mercenary and a "walking advertisement for one of Cheney's defense companies—like they just want us to be on TV all geared up in products." The conversation leads another soldier to privately comment later that, "The burden of this war falls disproportionately on the poor."

Faye Crawford, the mother of Sergeant Gauthreaux, wrestles with that point. She is now raising her son's 4-year-old son—he was a single father—and she says that sometimes in her darkest moments she has blamed herself for not having enough money to send her son to college. "If I could have sent him to college . . ." she begins, and her voice trails off as she chokes back tears. She knows, too, that her son loved what he did, and he believed that he was helping people in Iraq. "He would say, 'Mama, you should see their faces. They're so grateful.'" But Crawford wrestles with her son's sacrifice as the war fades from the front pages. "You hear that the economy is more important in the election than the war is," she says. "Sometimes I worry that people are already forgetting."

Strains. The evening that the team learned Gauthreaux had died, Del Valle contemplated getting out of the Army, imagining what his own death would do to his wife and daughter. Now home at Fort Hood since December, Del Valle, a native of Puerto Rico, has been promoted to the rank of command sergeant major. During his time in Iraq, he helped his own soldiers through some rough times and grew close to his Iraqi Army counterpart. Today, Del Valle is prepared to deploy again. "I think it would be kind of selfish for me to walk away from the Army now," he says.

The family strains on U.S. soldiers are immense, but Jones says troops are also helping another country rebuild itself and its families as well. "That matters a lot," he says. "I went over and trained a medical platoon. Those guys are really proficient now, and I'm proud about that," adds Jones, whose next assignment will be as a recruiter.

That will not be an easy job, he knows, meeting his numbers in the middle of a war. And he has wrestled with what he will tell potential recruits—how to encapsulate the experience of a soldier in the Army today. But he has settled on an answer. "The truth," he says. "All I can do is tell them the truth."

> *"It is not too late to make sure the government provides decent welfare to the troops who have borne the burden of combat."*

The U.S. Government Should Provide Better Care for Its Armed Forces Veterans

Linda Bilmes

Treating U.S. veterans should be a priority, asserts Linda Bilmes in the following viewpoint. The transition from active duty to civilian life has become a quagmire for unanticipated numbers of wounded veterans returning from Iraq, she claims. These veterans become enmeshed in a bureaucratic battle between the Department of Defense and the Department of Veterans Affairs, Bilmes maintains. Remedying these problems is necessary to provide for the welfare of those who bear the burden of war, she reasons. Harvard University professor Bilmes is coauthor of The Three Trillion Dollar War: The True Cost of the Iraq Conflict.

Linda Bilmes, "Soldiers Trapped in Limbo," *Boston Globe*, March 21, 2007, p. A9. Reproduced by permission of the author.

As you read, consider the following questions:

1. How many of those deployed to Iraq and Afghanistan have been officially listed as wounded, according to Bilmes?

2. What evidence does the author cite of a lack of continuity of care for wounded veterans?

3. In the author's opinion, what are three lessons to be learned from the Walter Reed scandal?

On the fourth anniversary [in March 2007] of the invasion of Iraq, one of the lasting images for Americans remains the squalid conditions at Walter Reed Army Medical Center. Who can forget the pictures of soldiers recently returned from the battle, trying to recover from horrific wounds while forced to keep fighting against dirt, mold, and bureaucracy? [Editor's Note: In February 2007, the *Washington Post* published articles that exposed cases of neglect at Walter Reed.]

The Real Culprit

The seeds of the Walter Reed scandal were sown in weak leadership, heavy reliance on outside contractors, and a failure to foresee the sheer number and severity of casualties. But the real culprit lies in a lack of trust between the Pentagon and the Department of Veterans Affairs. When a soldier is injured, the military decides whether he or she is fit to return to duty. If not, a second level of evaluation determines just how unfit he is. Soldiers awaiting this second level evaluation—including those at the Walter Reed outpatient clinic and scores of other military bases—are often trapped in limbo between military and veteran status.

Of the 1.4 million of service members deployed to the Iraq and Afghanistan wars, about 53,000 were officially listed as wounded or injured. Tens of thousands of others suffer from less visible wounds, such as traumatic brain injury, post-traumatic stress disorder, and debilitating chronic pain.

The military does not have enough health care practitioners to evaluate all soldiers before discharge. Some simply stay in the military, knowing that if they leave, they lose valuable housing and health care benefits, especially for their families. Others go to a VA [Veterans Administration] hospital for an evaluation, either because they gave up waiting or they aren't satisfied with the military evaluation and hope the VA will do better. As a consequence, the transition from active duty to veteran status becomes a quagmire instead of the seamless process desired by both departments.

This bureaucratic turf war extends beyond the wounded. More than 200,000 war veterans have already been treated at VA hospitals and clinics. But a penchant for privacy and outdated information technology means the Defense Department is unwilling and in some cases unable to provide medical records to the VA and thus to provide a continuity of care. Even when the VA gets the records, it often insists on repeating all the medical procedures and diagnostic tests before disability status can be granted. Many veterans travel 90 miles or more to reach the nearest VA medical facility. Even veterans already in a wheelchair must endure this prolonged, costly, and redundant process.

Soldiers injured in theater [field of operations] are supposedly able to apply for disability benefits *before* they are discharged. But to take advantage of the program a soldier must know when he is going to be discharged. Unfortunately, much of the force doesn't know when it will be discharged because of repeated deployments and "stop-loss" orders. Furthermore, National Guard and [Army] Reserve soldiers are excluded from the predischarge program.

The bureaucratic fumbling between the Department of Defense and the Department of Veterans Affairs also diverts the VA's stretched medical resources into claims processing and away from providing prompt, needed treatment.

Learning Simple Lessons

Here are some simple lessons from the Walter Reed scandal that will improve the lot of the 900,000 servicemen who are still deployed into the Iraq and Afghanistan wars:

First, the military should be required to give everyone a medical exam before discharge, and the Department of Defense should promptly transfer all records to the VA to expedite delivery of medical care and disability benefits.

Second, Veterans Affairs must hire thousands of additional mental health professionals and triage nurses, and double the number of local "veterans centers," which offer readjustment counseling in convenient neighborhood locations.

Third, the departments must work together to make the successful "Disability Benefits at Discharge" program into a workable option for all war veterans. This means sending more benefits experts to military bases, and expanding the program to include Reservists and National Guards.

Finally, the lack of planning that has characterized the war has led to overcrowded veteran facilities, waiting lists, and a backlog of pending disability claims. Needs of returning troops must be immediately analyzed and plans made for their return.

It may be too late to secure the peace and democracy in Iraq this war was supposed to achieve. But it is not too late to make sure the government provides decent welfare to the troops who have borne the burden of combat.

> "[The Veterans Administration] has received numerous accolades ... documenting the Department's leadership position in providing word-class health care to veterans."

The Veterans Administration Provides Excellent Care for Veterans of the Armed Forces

Michael J. Kussman

The Veterans Administration (VA) provides high-quality health care to America's veterans, argues Michael J. Kussman in the following viewpoint. The VA is, in fact, the leading provider of health care in the nation, he claims. For example, Kussman maintains, the VA maintains an award-winning computerized patient records system. Moreover, he asserts, the VA has expanded its services for veterans who suffer from post-traumatic stress disorder and other mental health disorders. To meet the demand for specialized medical care, the government must provide the VA with much needed resources, he reasons. Kussman, a former Army general, retired from the VA in May 2009.

Michael J. Kussman, "Written Statement of Michael J. Kussman, Acting Under Secretary for Health, Department of Veterans Affairs," House Committee on Appropriations Subcommittee on Military Construction, Veterans' Affairs and Related Agencies, March 6, 2007.

As you read, consider the following questions:

1. According to Kussman, how has the VA assisted severely injured service members from Iraq and Afghanistan?

2. In the author's opinion, how was the value of the VA's patient record system demonstrated following Hurricane Katrina?

3. In the author's view, how does Advanced Clinic Access promote the efficient flow of patients?

[The Veterans Health Administration] will continue to ensure that every seriously injured or ill serviceman or woman returning from combat in Operation Iraqi Freedom and Operation Enduring Freedom receives the treatment they need in a timely way.

Secretary [Jim] Nicholson announced plans to create a special Advisory Committee on Operation Iraqi Freedom/ Operation Enduring Freedom Veterans and Families. The panel, with membership including veterans, spouses, survivors, and parents of the latest generation of combat veterans, will report directly to the Secretary. Under its charter, the committee will focus on the concerns of all men and women with active military service in Operation Iraqi Freedom or Operation Enduring Freedom, but will pay particular attention to severely disabled veterans and their families.

Ensuring a Seamless Transition

VA [the Veterans Administration] launched an ambitious outreach initiative to ensure separating combat veterans know about the benefits and services available to them. During 2006 VA conducted over 8,500 briefings attended by more than 393,000 separating service members and returning reservists and National Guard members. The number of attendees was 20 percent higher in 2006 than it was in 2005 attesting to our improved outreach effort.

Additional pamphlet mailings following separation and briefings conducted at town hall meetings are sources of important information for returning National Guard members and reservists. VA has made a special effort to work with National Guard and reserve units to reach transitioning service members at demobilization sites and has trained recently discharged veterans to serve as National Guard Bureau liaisons in every state to assist their fellow combat veterans.

Each VA medical center has a designated point of contact to coordinate activities locally and to ensure the health care needs of returning service members and veterans are fully met. VA has distributed specific guidance to field staff to make sure the roles and functions of the points of contact and case managers are fully understood and that proper coordination of benefits and services occurs at the local level.

For combat veterans returning from Iraq and Afghanistan, their contact with VA often begins with priority scheduling for health care, and for the most seriously wounded, VA counselors visit their bedside in military wards before separation to assist them with their disability claims and ensure timely compensation payments when they leave active duty.

In an effort to assist wounded military members and their families, VA has placed workers at key military hospitals where severely injured service members from Iraq and Afghanistan are frequently sent for care. These include benefit counselors who help service members obtain VA services as well as social workers who facilitate health care coordination and discharge planning as service members transition from military to VA health care. Under this program, VA staff provides assistance at 10 military treatment facilities around the country, including Walter Reed Army Medical Center, the National Naval Medical Center Bethesda, the Naval Medical Center San Diego, and Womack Army Medical Center at Ft. Bragg.

Expanding Specialized Care

To further meet the need for specialized medical care for patients with service in Operation Iraqi Freedom and Operation Enduring Freedom, VA has expanded its four polytrauma centers in Minneapolis, Palo Alto, Richmond, and Tampa to encompass additional specialties to treat patients for multiple complex injuries. Our efforts are being expanded to 21 polytrauma network sites and clinic support teams around the country providing state-of-the-art treatment closer to injured veterans' homes. We have made training mandatory for all physicians and other key health care personnel on the most current approaches and treatment protocols for effective care of patients afflicted with brain injuries. Furthermore, we established a polytrauma call center in February 2006 to assist the families of our most seriously injured combat veterans and service members. This call center operates 24 hours a day, 7 days a week to answer clinical, administrative, and benefit inquiries from polytrauma patients and family members.

In addition, VA has significantly expanded its counseling and other medical care services for recently discharged veterans suffering from mental health disorders, including posttraumatic stress disorder. We have launched new programs, including dozens of new mental health teams based in VA medical facilities focused on early identification and management of stress-related disorders, as well as the recruitment of about 100 combat veterans as counselors to provide briefings to transitioning service members regarding military-related readjustment needs. . . .

Providing Quality Care

The resources we are requesting for VA's medical care program will allow us to strengthen our position as the Nation's leader in providing high-quality health care. VA has received numerous accolades from external organizations documenting the Department's leadership position in providing world-class

---

A Highly Ranked Health Care Leader

Veterans continued to rate the care they receive through the Department of Veterans Affairs health care system higher than other Americans rate private-sector health care....

In addition, VA remains a leader in medical research, developing the pacemaker, helping pioneer the CT [computed tomography] scan, and performing the first liver transplant, among other advances.

Donna Miles,
"VA Outranks Private Sector in Health Care Patient Satisfaction,"
American Forces Press Service, January 20, 2006.

---

health care to veterans. For example, our record of success in health care delivery is substantiated by the results of the 2006 American Customer Satisfaction Index (ACSI) survey. Conducted by the National Quality Research Center at the University of Michigan Business School, the ACSI survey found that customer satisfaction with VA's health care system increased last year [2006] and was higher than the private sector for the seventh consecutive year. The data revealed that inpatients at VA medical centers recorded a satisfaction level of 84 out of a possible 100 points, or 10 points higher than the rating for inpatient care provided by the private-sector health care industry. VA's rating of 82 for outpatient care was 8 points better than the private sector.

Citing VA's leadership role in transforming health care in America, Harvard University recognized the Department's computerized patient records system by awarding VA the prestigious "Innovations in American Government Award" in 2006. Our electronic health records have been an important element in making VA health care the benchmark for 294 measures of disease prevention and treatment in the U.S. The value of this system was clearly demonstrated when every patient medical record from the areas devastated by Hurricane Katrina was made available to all VA health care providers throughout the Nation within 100 hours of the time the storm made landfall. Veterans were able to quickly resume their treatments, refill their prescriptions, and get the care they needed because of the electronic health records system—a real, functioning health information exchange that has been a proven success resulting in improved quality of care. It can serve as a model for the health care industry as the Nation moves forward with the public/private effort to develop a Nationwide Health Information Network.

Recognized Excellence

The Department also received an award from the American Council for Technology for our collaboration with the Department of Defense on the Bidirectional Health Information Exchange program. This innovation permits the secure, real-time exchange of medical record data between the two departments, thereby avoiding duplicate testing and surgical procedures. It is an important step forward in making the transition from active duty to civilian life as smooth and seamless as possible.

In its July 17, 2006, edition, *BusinessWeek* featured an article about VA health care titled "The Best Medical Care in the U.S." This article outlines many of the Department's accomplishments that have helped us achieve our position as the leading provider of health care in the country, such as higher quality of care than the private sector, our nearly perfect rate of prescription accuracy, and the most advanced computerized medical records system in the Nation. Similar high praise for VA's health care system was documented in the September 4, 2006, edition of *Time* magazine in an article titled "How

[Veterans'] Hospitals Became the Best [in Health Care]." In addition, a study conducted by Harvard Medical School concluded that federal hospitals, including those managed by VA, provide the best care available for some of the most common life-threatening illnesses such as congestive heart failure, heart attack, and pneumonia. Their research results were published in the December 11, 2006, edition of the *Annals of Internal Medicine.*

These external acknowledgments of the superior quality of VA health care reinforce the Department's own findings. We use two primary measures of health care quality—clinical practice guidelines index and prevention index. These measures focus on the degree to which VA follows nationally recognized guidelines and standards of care that the medical literature has proven to be directly linked to improved health outcomes for patients. Our performance on the clinical practice guidelines index, which focuses on high-prevalence and high-risk diseases that have a significant impact on veterans' overall health status, is expected to grow to 85 percent in 2008, or a 1 percentage point rise over the level we expect to achieve this year. As an indicator aimed at primary prevention and early detection recommendations dealing with immunizations and screenings, the prevention index will be maintained at our existing high level of performance of 88 percent.

Improving Access to Care

With the resources requested for medical care in 2008, the Department will be able to continue our exceptional performance dealing with access to health care—96 percent of primary care appointments will be scheduled within 30 days of patients' desired date, and 95 percent of specialty care appointments will be scheduled within 30 days of patients' desired date. We will minimize the number of new enrollees waiting for their first appointment. We reduced this number by 94 percent from May 2006 to January 2007, to a little more than 1,400, and we will continue to place strong emphasis on lowering, and then holding, the waiting list to as low a level as possible.

An important component of our overall strategy to improve access and timeliness of service is the implementation on a national scale of Advanced Clinic Access, an initiative that promotes the efficient flow of patients by predicting and anticipating patient needs at the time of their appointment. This involves assuring that specific medical equipment is available, arranging for tests that should be completed either prior to, or at the time of, the patient's visit, and ensuring all necessary health information is available. This program optimizes clinical scheduling so that each appointment or inpatient service is most productive. In addition, this reduces unnecessary appointments, allowing for relatively greater workload and increased patient-directed scheduling. . . .

I am very proud to be leading the Veterans Health Administration at this time. I am proud of our system and its accomplishments, and I look forward to working with the members of this committee to continue the Department's tradition of providing timely, high-quality health care to those who have helped defend and preserve freedom around the world.

> *"There is a clearly defined need for re-view and revision of how rules of en-gagement (ROE) are conceptualized . . . as well as how we as leaders train soldiers to make the right decisions."*

The U.S. Military Should Reconsider the Rules of Engagement for Twenty-first Century Warfare

Louis V. Netherland

The challenges faced by armed forces in Iraq and Afghanistan require that military policy makers revisit the rules of engagement (ROE), which govern the use of deadly force, asserts Major Louis V. Netherland in the following viewpoint. Before drafting ROE, he claims, policy makers must consider the situation on the ground in Iraq and Afghanistan. For example, innocent civilians are often located in the combat zone and visibility of the threat may be limited, Netherland maintains. Revised ROE need not encourage more liberal use of deadly force but acknowledge the complex variables twenty-first-century soldiers face, he argues. At the time of this writing, Netherland was a U.S. army

Louis V. Netherland, "21st-Century Rules of Engagement," *Armor*, vol. 115, January–February 2006, pp. 23–25. Copyright © 2006 U.S. Army Armor Center. Reproduced by permission of the author.

commander. Netherland is an Armor Officer in the U.S. Army, and deployed most recently to Afghanistan from 2007–2008 as an advisor to the Afghan National Police in Laghman Province. He continues to serve the Army as a Foreign Area Officer to Latin America.

As you read, consider the following questions:

1. In Netherland's view, what are the good news and the bad news about the exercise he uses to open his viewpoint?

2. What compounds the challenge in identifying supportable rules concerning the use of deadly force, in the author's opinion?

3. According to the author, in what law is the legal precedence regarding the use of deadly force grounded?

In producing this updated foreword for my article, I cannot stress enough the importance of the reader reflecting upon the original publishing date and placing that within the historical context during which it was written.

For those on the ground in Iraq at the start of 2005, there was presented a very different set of circumstances and challenges facing the U.S. military than those that exist today. The complexities of fighting the first large-scale counterinsurgency since the Vietnam era were evident in virtually every aspect of strategic planning and policy making conducted by the United States. Even at the time this article was originally published, the U.S. Army was still almost a full year away from releasing a new Counterinsurgency Field Manual. In short, there was no playbook, and U.S. forces found themselves adapting to the situation on the ground, quite literally, under fire.

Of the countless dimensions through which an effective strategy had to be developed, one of the most important was the adoption of appropriate Rules of Engagement (ROE) and

Rules of the Use of Force (RUF) that provided for the protection of both U.S. forces and the civilian populations of Afghanistan and Iraq. For those upon whom the task fell, drafting these ROE/RUF was a balancing act of tremendous proportions. On the one hand, the ROE had to be liberal enough to protect U.S. and Iraqi forces and civilians in areas where suicide bombers, improvised explosive devices (IEDs), and other unconventional forms of attack were commonplace. On the other hand, the ROE had to be rigid enough to prevent tragedies in which innocent civilians could be mistaken for a threat and killed or wounded.

By late 2005, the U.S. had met with mixed success in the creation and implementation of effective ROE/RUF, but there was no clear-cut solution to every scenario; err too much on one side or the other of caution and a tragedy occurred either way. Those who sought a one-size-fits-all solution found themselves adrift. It was in this environment that a necessary and constructive debate was taking place among the U.S. Armed Forces attempting to address this issue for the long term, and it was within this debate that "21st Century Rules of Engagement" was published.

The solution to creating effective ROE/RUF in the constantly evolving environment of a counterinsurgency was eventually found, as with most things, somewhere in the middle. To simply apply one set of all-encompassing ROE to an entire theater would never work. ROE/RUF must be developed, monitored, and adjusted by the unit on the ground that understands the dynamics of the environment in which it is working. The ROE are then most effective, because they are flexible enough to meet the changing needs of the situation, and therefore work toward an end state: the eventual return of a safe and secure environment for the people.

At a dusty checkpoint on a February afternoon, a squad of young cavalry scouts was in a challenging situation. As an unidentified civilian male approached their checkpoint on foot, the squad leader gave the order to halt when the man closed to within 100 meters of the barrier. The man, who shifted his hands to his front jacket pockets, continued to walk for approximately 15 meters, where he stopped in the middle of the road, glancing nervously from side to side. The squad leader called for the man to remove his hands from his pockets—there was a noticeable bulge beneath his jacket at chest level. The man kept his hands concealed, now shifting forward and backward a few steps and mumbling under his breath. From covered positions, the scouts trained their weapons on the man as the squad leader called back to the tactical operations center (TOC) with the report. For the next 10 minutes, a standoff ensued—the scouts assumed the man was a suicide bomber who had intended to get closer to the checkpoint before detonating, only to now find himself unable to go any farther, forward or backward, without being shot. Maybe he had lost his nerve; maybe the device had malfunctioned; maybe he wasn't a threat at all. The man began to call out loudly, falling to his knees and then rising again in a quick walk toward the checkpoint. The scouts called again and again for him to halt. The squad leader froze in a moment of uncertainty. When the man closed to within 20 meters of the barrier, a young private squeezed off three rounds at center mass. The shots seemed to jar loose the air of gridlock, and another two privates first class engaged their M16s as well. The unidentified man fell dead—15 meters short of the checkpoint.

That's when end of exercise (ENDEX) was called.

A Good News, Bad News Exercise

The checkpoint had not been on the outskirts of the green zone or the mountain passes of eastern Afghanistan, but was instead located in Training Area 3, Fort Knox, Kentucky. The scouts were not from the 2d Armored Cavalry Regiment, 1st Cavalry Division, or 3d Infantry Division, but were 19D10 one-station unit training (OSUT) soldiers from the 5th Squadron, 15th U.S. Cavalry, most with less than 120 days in the Army. In the after-action review (AAR) that followed the incident, the scouts-to-be were concerned: "Was it OK that we shot him?" "I thought I saw something under his jacket, but I can't be sure." "Did we let him get too close to us?" "Should we have shot him if he turned to run away?" And the question on every mind: "Would we get in trouble if this had been real?"

In light of these questions, one can't help but see both the good news and bad news of the situation. The good news is the privates genuinely cared about doing the right thing, and demonstrated that they are smart, motivated, responsible young men. The bad news is they were concerned with "getting in trouble," which caused hesitancy; that hesitancy would have likely gotten them killed or seriously wounded.

A Useful Dialogue

Situations, such as the one illustrated above, as well as others, were among topics discussed by a panel of U.S. Army and Air Force Staff Judge Advocates and Federal Law Enforcement Officers during a recent visit to Fort Knox as part of the Rules of Engagement/Rules of the Use of Force Tactical Training Seminar. The seminar, similar to those presented at Special Operations Central Command (SOCCENT), Fort Stewart, Georgia, the United States Military Academy, and the FBI Academy, serves to familiarize attendees with legal and tactical lessons learned by the U.S. Department of Justice (DOJ) and the civilian law enforcement community concerning the application of use of force—particularly deadly force.

Such dialogue is useful given the fact that operations within the contemporary operating environment (COE) are increasingly encompassing tasks that bear resemblance to what law enforcement officers face each day. Additionally, the historical record of the U.S. Armed Forces in understanding

20 Different Answers Demonstrate Ambiguity

The rules of engagement have one fundamental under-pinning, and that is that every soldier or marine has the right to self-defense. That's the first and foremost element of the rules of engagement. And every marine and soldier can tell you that. They have a little card and they can tell you what the card says.

The problem with the rules of engagement is that if you give those same group of young people a hypothetical circumstance and [ask] them how they would react to it, you get 20 different answers.

Gary Myers, "Rules of Engagement,"
Frontline, February 19, 2008. www.pbs.org.

and applying threat recognition, rules of self-defense, and use of appropriate defensive postures in nontraditional tactical environments, arguably leaves much room for improvement. There is a clearly defined need for review and revision of how rules of engagement (ROE) are conceptualized, developed, and published, as well as how we as leaders train soldiers to make the right decisions in defending themselves and protecting others.

Discussing the Use of Force

Guest speakers at the seminar discussed the foundational knowledge regarding the full spectrum of use of force issues and debates. The development of use of force policies in a given theater [field] of operations is a detailed process that must consider national policy, the laws of land warfare, and the characteristics of the operational environment to achieve an end product for implementation. The challenge exists in identifying legally supportable rules concerning the use of deadly force that remain tactically sound enough to avoid placing a soldier's life in unnecessary danger. Compounding this challenge is the verbiage used as the start point of most ROE, "You may use force, including deadly force, when you reasonably believe yourself or others to be in imminent danger of death or serious bodily harm." Such language leaves the man on the ground with the overarching question: "What constitutes imminent danger?"

The difficulties of developing and managing ROE/rules of the use of force (RUF) issues led some commanders to impose certain control measures to mitigate virtually any threat of perceived impropriety. Many of these measures contributed to, rather than alleviated, confusion amongst the rank and file of deployed personnel, and resulted in ROE/RUF policies that put soldiers at risk and security in question. The seminar highlighted some of these policies in citing various real-world examples from across the front. These examples extended along the spectrum of response: prohibiting troops on guard duty from inserting magazines into their wells; use of "minimum force necessary"; guarded authorization of "use of deadly force as a last resort"; and provisions against shooting a fleeing hostile actor from the scene of an attack.

Such examples represent a larger trend toward imbalance between the risk-averse and the risk-inclined. This imbalance is weighted by a latent fear of using force, paranoia of the "accidental" discharge, and a dual misunderstanding of both the dynamics of a deadly force encounter and the laws justifying such force. In discussing these issues, the seminar focused on providing an understanding of both the applicable law and the dynamics of such encounters as they relate to one another. A greater appreciation of this relationship is generally accepted as the fundamental building block on which tactically minded, legally supportable ROE may be drafted for use in theaters of conflict.

Legal Precedence

Not surprisingly, much of the legal precedence regarding the use of deadly force is grounded in civilian, not military, law. The seminar focused on historic decisions that helped to establish one of the key legal considerations in drafting any ROE; a rigorous balance must exist between the perception of a reasonable response to a threat, and how unique conditions of the event are weighed in passing final judgment. For example, in *Graham v. Connor* [of 1989], the judicial opinion addressed the fact that determining the reasonableness of a shoot/no-shoot encounter is not reliably accomplished through the sterile eyes of a detached observer, but rather to be balanced within the physical and mental circumstances of the incident: ". . . such reasonableness must be judged from the perspective of a reasonable officer on the scene, rather than with the 20/20 vision of hindsight . . . the calculus of reasonableness must embody allowance for the fact that police officers are often forced to make split-second judgments about the amount of force that is necessary in a particular situation in circumstances that are tense, uncertain, and rapidly evolving."

In [*Brown v. United States* in 1921], the published opinion cautioned against the idea that law enforcement officers must fully exercise the capability to pause and analyze the intent of an attacker before using deadly force: "Detached Reflection cannot be demanded in the presence of an uplifted knife." The seminar then posed the subsequent dilemma as to how, then, certain ROE still demand such detached reflection in the presence of an uplifted AK-47?

The Dynamics of Deadly Force

With legal precedence supporting the notion that reasonableness of action is weighed against the circumstances of the encounter, it is helpful to devote some thought as to just how varied those circumstances may be. The dynamics of a deadly force encounter are part of a psychologically and physiologically complex process, and it is indeed a process; a systematic series of events that unfold both consciously and subconsciously in the mind's eye of the soldier. That process requires the soldier to first recognize the threat, then choose the appropriate level of response for the threat, and finally implement that response, all in a matter of seconds. Even under the best conditions, it is a challenging and highly charged event. Add to this the variables of: limited visibility; innocent civilians intermixed within the battlespace; rapid and unpredictable movement by shooter and target(s); the life and death stress of sudden, close, personal violence; and any myriad of sudden, unexpected circumstances, and such encounters become even more demanding. What remains is the fundamental importance of ROE/RUF policy makers understanding the intricacies of the tactical situation on the ground before drafting regulations that decrease overall security and threaten the safety of both soldiers and civilians.

It is important to note that this article is not an argument for more liberal ROE that ignore the equally complex and sensitive political-military environment of a combat zone. There is no mistaking that the job of those who draft and approve ROE for use in theater involves an extraordinary balance of issues of monumental importance. Critics voiced pronounced concern that the seminar advocated and encouraged a trigger-happy mentality amongst attendees; that it created a dangerous opportunity for an individual to cover himself in a protective blanket of the circumstantial. But to the contrary, the real message encouraged everyone to think more broadly and more tactically about security and security-related policies and procedures. The true value of the information presented encouraged a positive change in the cultural mind-set of officers and noncommissioned officers, leaders who might otherwise be reluctant to break apart the 20th-century formula for drafting ROE and rethink to reconfigure all of the factors that embody such policy. The 21st-century battlefield demands nothing less.

> "[Selective conscientious objection] would serve ... as a much-needed internal moral compass for U.S. warmaking."

Selective Conscientious Objection to Military Service Should Be Legalized

Gregory D. Foster

Selective conscientious objection should be a legal option for soldiers who oppose immoral wars, argues Gregory D. Foster in the following viewpoint. When U.S. presidents expand their warmaking powers in violation of the U.S. Constitution, soldiers should have the choice not to obey them, he asserts. Moreover, Foster claims, soldiers should have the right not to serve irresponsible governments. Legalizing selective conscientious objection would not only protect soldiers, he reasons, but also restrain the use of military force. Foster, a professor at National Defense University, is a West Point graduate and decorated veteran of the Vietnam War.

Gregory D. Foster, "One War at a Time," *America*, vol. 199, November 17, 2008, pp. 16–18.

As you read, consider the following questions:

1. What does Foster argue is perversely ironic about those who profess opposition to war?

2. Why has the constitutional superstructure failed to protect those in uniform, in the author's opinion?

3. In the author's view, how does America's volunteer military underscore the need for selective conscientious objection?

It is perversely ironic that we Americans, even those who profess opposition to war, generally glorify the people who fight our wars. In contrast, we usually treat conscientious objectors with undisguised disdain. They are, in the minds of many, malingerers, shirkers, cowards, even traitors, not models of principled rectitude and courage.

Not until the day comes when conscientious objectors are seen to be contributing to society rather than evading sacrifice will they be accorded acceptance and respect. And only then will the possibility of discrediting and eliminating war as a preferred instrument of statecraft become a realizable ideal. The path to that end lies in the legitimization and institutionalization of selective conscientious objection: the currently unaccepted right of those in uniform to formally express their objection to, and refusal to serve in, particular wars.

The Current Conscientious Objection Law

At present, such selective opposition is proscribed by law. The legal provision covering conscientious objection, found in the Military Selective Service Act, reads: "Nothing contained in this title . . . shall be construed to require any person to be subject to combatant training and service in the armed forces of the United States who, by reason of religious training and belief, is conscientiously opposed to participation in war in any form."

The key phrase "war in any form" is further clarified in Pentagon policy: "An individual who desires to choose the war in which he or she will participate is not a Conscientious Objector under the law. The individual's objection must be to all wars rather than a specific war." Thus, an individual opposed to serving in a particular war—one badly conceived or wrongfully conducted for instance—must, in order to be honorably discharged or assigned to noncombatant duties, demonstrate convincingly that he/she opposes *all* war, or be willing to face dire consequences (court-martial and possibly prison), or take more drastic action—like deserting, going absent without leave, missing troop movement or disobeying an order. For someone not opposed to all war (especially wars of necessity) and otherwise willing to serve this country in uniform, the current situation poses an intractable dilemma that argues for legalizing selective conscientious objection.

The Reasons for a New Law

The need for selective objection is rooted first in the fact that the machinery of war in this country is seriously broken. All recent U.S. presidents have sought to expand and exercise their war-making powers at the expense of Congresses that consistently have favored political and ideological loyalties over their constitutional duty to check and balance executive excess. Congresses have gone to extraordinary lengths to avoid the politically risky responsibility for declaring wars and then for ending them. And the Supreme Court, abjuring its prerogative for judicial review, has resolutely refused to rule on the legality of particular wars. Thus the constitutional superstructure meant to tether the dogs of war provides precious little protection to those in uniform, the pawns of war.

The need for selective objection also rests on the contractual relationship between military personnel, the government, and society. The written contract governing the men and women in uniform is their oath of office, which binds adher-

An Immoral and Illegal Distinction

[The] distinction between General and Selective Conscientious Objection [CO] and the military's refusal to acknowledge the latter presents the soldier with a crisis of conscience regarding whether to follow orders and participate in what he determines to be an immoral and illegal war or to follow the dictates of his conscience, disobey orders, refuse to fight and face serious disciplinary action. Upon analysis, it is clear that the military's position on CO status is morally and legally untenable—inconsistent with the demands both of morality and of law.

Camillo Bica, "A Crisis of Conscience:
Conscientious Objection, Law and Morality,"
Truthout, December 9, 2008. www.truthout.org.

ents to support unreservedly and defend the Constitution and obligates them to obey the lawful orders of the president and other superior officers. All in uniform therefore give dutiful, silent obedience and tacitly accept restrictions on individual rights in return for lawful, constitutional behavior by those above them in the chain of command.

But there also is a tacit social contract of mutual rights, obligations and expectations. This unwritten contract implies that in return for giving dutiful obedience and giving up certain rights, military personnel have a right to expect and receive from their superiors behavior that is not only constitutional and legal, but also ethical, competent and accountable. Where government (including the military chain of command) fails on any of these counts, the contract, and with it the reciprocal obligation for dutiful obedience and forgone rights, is broken.

An Unexamined Notion

Two other factors underscore the need for selective objection. Most notably, contemporary wars are no longer wars of necessity; they are, without exception, wars of choice. Yet conscientious objection is predicated on the unexamined notion that the wars we fight are wars of necessity, involving a one-way relationship of government rights and individual obligations. When wars of choice are the norm, however, where survival is not at stake and emergency conditions do not prevail, the reverse of this relationship is called for: one in which government is obligated to act responsibly and competently, while individuals in uniform retain the right not to serve (or honor their commitment) when government fails to meet its obligations.

Another factor underscoring the need for selective conscientious objection is, counterintuitively, America's volunteer military. Historically, conscientious objection has been tolerated principally because of its relationship to conscription. Some would argue that conscientious objection does not and should not apply to volunteers who have joined the military of their own volition, eyes wide open, knowing full well what to expect. Of all people, they should be willing to forsake certain rights, defer unquestioningly to higher authority and face the ultimate sacrifice.

It is instructive, however, to remind ourselves that Title 10 of the United States Code specifies the mission of the U.S. Army as not simply to wage war, but to be "capable . . . of preserving the peace and security, and providing for the defense, of the United States." Arguably, therefore, the law is on the side of those in uniform who volunteer to defend their country as a matter of necessity, not to fight wars of choice wrongly undertaken or wrongfully prosecuted.

Serving Three Purposes

Selective conscientious objection would serve three major purposes. First, it would protect military personnel by according them the most fundamental right any party to a social contract deserves: the right to withdraw from that contract (or seek redress) if the other party—the government in general, the military in particular—breaks or fails to honor it.

Second, it would serve, in the absence of conscription, as a much-needed internal moral compass for U.S. war-making. Ideally, conscription serves this purpose creating stakeholders throughout society—especially among elites otherwise disinclined to serve or have their offspring serve—who are willing to scrutinize and restrain the use of military force. But since conscription seems destined to remain a vestige of America's past, selective objection would be a surrogate, the presumption being that legalizing the practice would embolden those in uniform—war's ultimate stakeholders—who object to wrongful and wrongheaded wars to express their opposition formally. At some point, a critical mass of such internal opposition might be reached that would force lawmakers and society to take notice and act.

Third, selective objection would place a premium on deliberative reason, rather than religious (or religious-like) belief, and thereby serve the embedded aim of producing individuals in uniform who are civically engaged and civically competent, not simply true-believing followers of religious or ideological dogma.

If ever there was a time to put a system of selective conscientious objection in place, it is now. Otherwise, individuals of conscience who are courageous enough to step outside the obedient herd will continue to attract undeserved opprobrium, war will persist as our eternal lot, and we will have only our own silent indifference to blame.

Periodical Bibliography

The following articles have been selected to supplement the diverse views presented in this chapter.

Michael Barbero	"Meeting the Challenges of the Operational Environment," *Infantry Magazine*, November/December 2008.
Camillo Bica	"A Crisis of Conscience: Conscientious Objection, Law and Morality," Truthout, December 9, 2008. www.truthout.org.
Kari Huus	"Gut Check: Iraq War's Impact at Home," MSNBC.com, October 15, 2007. www.msnbc.com.
Joseph B. Mackey	"Reclaiming the In-Service Conscientious Objection Program: Proposals for Creating a Meaningful Limitation to the Claim of Conscientious Objection," *Army Lawyer*, August 2008.
Christopher Moraff	"Putting a Stop to Stop Loss," *In These Times*, May 2009.
Gary Myers	"The Rules of Engagement," *Frontline*, February 19, 2008. www.pbs.org.
Paul Robinson	"Ethics Training and Development in the Military," *Parameters*, Spring 2007.
Kirk Semple	"The Reach of War: Longer Duty Leaves Forces Disappointed but Stoic," *New York Times*, April 13, 2007.
Ann Scott Tyson	"Heavy Troop Deployments Are Called Major Risk," *Washington Post*, April 2, 2008.
Hans A. Von Spakovsky and Roman Buhler	"Disenfranchised over There; Let's Defend the Voting Rights of Those Who Defend Us," *Weekly Standard*, vol. 13, no. 33, May 12, 2008.

For Further Discussion

Chapter 1

1. Karl-Heinz Kamp claims that the preemptive use of armed forces is sometimes justified because evidence of a political group's or nation's hostile intent may come too late for self-defense. Michael S. Rozeff disagrees, arguing that nothing justifies preemptive force. What rhetorical strategies does each author use to support his claim? Which do you find more persuasive?

2. Gregory L. Cantwell argues that U.S. armed forces are well-suited for nation building. Peter Allen believes that the opposite is true. How do the authors' affiliations inform their rhetoric? Do you think this makes their arguments more or less persuasive?

3. Although Michael B. Oren and David Herbert agree that Somali piracy is a problem, the authors disagree over the seriousness of the threat and, therefore, the need for an armed forces response. What evidence does each author use to support the method he believes will best mitigate Somali piracy? Which do you find more persuasive?

4. Derek Reveron contends that armed forces are well-equipped to respond to disasters. Do you think Reveron adequately addresses concerns that the armed forces might abuse their role in disaster relief?

5. What evidence does Amy Goodman use to support her argument that armed forces might be used to quell domestic unrest in the United States? Do you find this evidence persuasive?

6. Of the roles of the armed forces debated by the authors in this chapter, which do you think is the most important?

Chapter 2

1. Bill Maxwell believes that reinstating the draft is necessary to improve the quality of recruits. Walter Y. Oi claims that an all-volunteer force is the most equitable way to staff a military. Which viewpoint do you find more persuasive?

2. James Kitfield and Nick Turse agree that recruiters face significant challenges in meeting their recruiting goals. The authors dispute, however, how recruiters are addressing these challenges. What rhetorical strategies does each author use to support his claim? Which do you find more persuasive?

3. Of the concerns about who should or should not serve in the military expressed by the authors in this chapter, which do you believe is the most important to address? Explain.

Chapter 3

1. Robert M. Gates argues that defense resources should be used to fight the current enemy: insurgents, guerrillas, and terrorists. He claims that conventional armies are not a likely threat. Charles J. Dunlap Jr. claims that U.S. armed forces should be prepared for an attack by a conventional army since failure to do so would be devastating. What evidence does each author provide to support his claim? Which evidence do you find more persuasive?

2. Robert Higgs believes that the nature of the relationship between private defense contractors, the government, and the military has created a pattern of corruption. President Barack Obama, however, is more optimistic. He claims that oversight reforms can eliminate waste. Do you think that Obama's reform strategies address Higgs's concerns?

Chapter 4

1. Gordon Lubold claims that long tours of duty have taken too great a toll on U.S. soldiers. Anna Mulrine does not dispute that long tours of duty put a strain on U.S. soldiers, but she asserts that the belief that they are doing good mitigates the stress. Do you think that these soldiers finding a way to manage the stress justifies continuing their long tours of duty? What in the viewpoints supports your view?

2. Linda Bilmes and Michael J. Kussman disagree about the quality of care provided to U.S. veterans. Do you think any of Kussman's suggestions to improve care of veterans will overcome Bilmes's objections?

3. Louis V. Netherland believes that the current rules of engagement do not take into consideration the situations soldiers face in Iraq and Afghanistan and thus should be reevaluated. What rhetorical strategy does he use to introduce his argument? Do you find it persuasive?

4. Gregory D. Foster argues that conscientious objection should be expanded to include specific conflicts that a soldier believes violate the U.S. Constitution. What evidence does he provide to support his claim? Do you find it persuasive?

5. Michael J. Kussman, Louis V. Netherland, and Gregory D. Foster have all served or are currently serving in the armed forces. Does this make their viewpoints more or less persuasive?

Organizations to Contact

The editors have compiled the following list of organizations concerned with the issues debated in this book. The descriptions are derived from materials provided by the organizations. All have publications or information available for interested readers. The list was compiled on the date of publication of the present volume; the information provided here may change. Be aware that many organizations take several weeks or longer to respond to inquiries, so allow as much time as possible.

American Civil Liberties Union (ACLU)
125 Broad Street, 18th Floor, New York, NY   10004-2400
(212) 549-2500
e-mail: aclu@aclu.org
Web site: www.aclu.org

The American Civil Liberties Union (ACLU) is a national organization that champions American civil rights. The organization maintains the position that government expediency and national security should not compromise fundamental civil liberties. It publishes and distributes policy statements, pamphlets, and press releases, including the reports *Soldiers of Misfortune: Abusive U.S. Military Recruitment and Failures to Protect Child Soldiers* and *No Real Threat: The Pentagon Secret Database on Peaceful Protest*, which are available on its Web site.

American Enterprise Institute (AEI)
1150 Seventeenth Street NW, Washington, DC   20036
(202) 862-5800 • fax: (202) 862-7177
Web site: www.aei.org

The American Enterprise Institute (AEI) is an organization dedicated to preserving limited government, private enterprise, and strong national defense. The institute's main areas of research include economic policy, social and political studies, and defense and foreign policy. AEI publishes the bimonthly magazine *American Enterprise*. It also publishes articles and commentary on issues related to the military and the use of armed force, many of which are available on its Web site.

Brookings Institution

1775 Massachusetts Avenue NW, Washington, DC   20036
(202) 797-6000 • fax: (202) 797-6004
e-mail: brookinfo@brook.edu
Web site: www.brook.edu

Founded in 1927, the Brookings Institution conducts research and analyzes global events and their impact on the United States and U.S. foreign policy. It publishes the quarterly *Brookings Review* and numerous books and research papers on foreign policy. Its Web site publishes editorials, papers, testimony, reports, and articles written by institute scholars, including "War, Profits, and the Vacuum of Law: Privatized Military Firms and International Law," "Increasing the Size and Power of the U.S. Military," and "Nobody Wants a Draft, but What If We Need One?"

Cato Institute

1000 Massachusetts Avenue NW
Washington, DC   20001-5403
(202) 842-0200 • fax: (202) 842-3490
Web site: www.cato.org

The Cato Institute is a libertarian public policy research foundation dedicated to peace and limited government intervention in foreign affairs. It publishes numerous reports and periodicals including *Policy Analysis* and *Cato Policy Review*, both of which discuss U.S. policy in regional conflicts. Its Web site contains a searchable database of institute articles, news, and commentary, including "Congress and the Power of War and Peace" and "The Wages of War."

Center for Defense Information (CDI)

1779 Massachusetts Avenue NW
Washington, DC 20036-2109
(202) 332-0600 • fax: (202) 462-4559
e-mail: info@cdi.org
Web site: www.cdi.org

The Center for Defense Information (CDI) is a nonpartisan organization that researches global security. It provides information to policy makers and the general public about security policy, global hot spots, and defense budgeting. It publishes the monthly *Defense Monitor*, which contains many articles and op-ed pieces on the composition of U.S. armed forces, weapons, nation building, defense spending, and other issues related to the armed forces.

Center for Strategic and International Studies (CSIS)

1800 K Street NW, Washington, DC 20006
(202) 887-0200 • fax: (202) 775-3199
Web site: www.csis.org

The Center for Strategic and International Studies (CSIS) is a public policy research institution that specializes in the areas of U.S. domestic and foreign policy, national security, and economic policy. The center analyzes world crisis situations and recommends U.S. military and defense policies. Its publications report on issues of interest to the center. Its Web site has a searchable database of news, articles, testimony, and reports including *Armed Nation Building* and *The Changing Challenges of U.S. Defense Spending*.

Center on Conscience & War (CCW)

1830 Connecticut Avenue NW, Washington, DC 20009
(202) 483-2220 • fax: (202) 483-1246
e-mail: ccw@centeronconscience.org
Web site: www.centeronconscience.com

The Center on Conscience & War (CCW), formerly the National Interreligious Service Board for Conscientious Objectors (NISBCO), was formed in 1940 by an association of religious bodies. CCW works to defend and extend the rights of conscientious objectors. The center is committed to supporting all those who question participation in war. It publishes the newsletter *The Reporter for Conscience' Sake*, issues of which are available on its Web site.

Committee Opposed to Militarism and the Draft (COMD)

PO Box 15195, San Diego, CA 92175
(760) 753-7518 • (619) 265-1369
e-mail: comd@comdsd.org
Web site: www.comdsd.org

The Committee Opposed to Militarism and the Draft (COMD) defines itself as an antimilitarism organization "that also challenges the institution of the military, its effect on society, its budget, its role abroad and at home, and the racism, sexism and homophobia that are inherent in the armed forces and Selective Service System." It directs its focus on community education, youth outreach, and direct action. The printable pamphlets *Teach Peace: Make Schools Military-Free Zones* and *High School Students' Rights* are available on its Web site.

Council on Foreign Relations

The Harold Pratt House, 58 East Sixty-Eighth Street, New
York, NY 10065
(212) 434-9400 • fax: (212) 434-9800
Web site: www.cfr.org

The Council on Foreign Relations (CFR) specializes in foreign affairs and studies the international aspects of American political and economic policies and problems. Its journal *Foreign Affairs*, published five times a year, includes analyses of current conflicts around the world. Its Web site publishes editorials, interviews, and articles including "The Humanitarian Transformation: Expanding Global Intervention Capacity" and "Enhancing U.S Preventive Action."

Crimes of War Project

1325 G Street NW, Suite 730, Washington, DC   20005
(202) 638-0230
e-mail: office@crimesofwar.org
Web site: www.crimesofwar.org

The Crimes of War Project is a collaboration of journalists, lawyers, and scholars dedicated to raising public awareness of the laws of war. The project publishes *Crimes of War* magazine, recent issues of which are available on its Web site, as are essays and reports including "Iraq and the 'Bush Doctrine' of Pre-emptive Self-Defense."

Iraq and Afghanistan Veterans of America (IAVA)

292 Madison Avenue, 10th Floor, New York, NY   10017
(212) 982-9699 • fax: (212) 982-8645
Web site: http://iava.org

Iraq and Afghanistan Veterans of America (IAVA) is a nonprofit advocacy organization dedicated to veterans who have served in the Iraq and Afghanistan wars and their families. On its Web site, IAVA publishes issue briefs, news, videos, and press releases on issues that concern veterans of the wars in Iraq and Afghanistan.

RAND Corporation

1776 Main Street, PO Box 2138
Santa Monica, CA   90407-2138
(310) 393-0411 • fax: (310) 393-4818
Web site: www.rand.org

The RAND Corporation is a nonprofit institution that helps improve policy and decision making through research and analysis. In addition to a broad range of topics, the corporation studies national security and international affairs and has published numerous books and other publications on these topics, many of which are available on the RAND Web site, including *How Have Deployments During the War on Terrorism Affected Reenlistment?* and *Real Threats, Real Fears, Real Defenses.*

Servicemembers Legal Defense Network (SLDF)
PO Box 65301, Washington, DC   20035-5301
(202) 328-3244 • fax: (202) 797-1635
e-mail: sldn@sldn.org
Web site: www.sldn.org

The Servicemembers Legal Defense Network (SLDF) is dedicated to ending discrimination against and harassment of military personnel affected by the military's "Don't Ask, Don't Tell" (DADT) policy. On its Web site, SLDF publishes articles and commentary on DADT, including "Honor All Who Want to Serve" and "Bring Equality to Military Service." It also maintains a DADT blog and posts video interviews and speeches and updates on DADT legislation.

U.S. Department of Defense
Office of Public Communication
Assistant Secretary of Defense for Public Affairs
1400 Defense Pentagon, Washington, DC   20310-1400
(703) 428-0711
Web site: www.defense.gov

The U.S. Department of Defense is the agency within the U.S. government charged with providing armed protection for the country as a whole. The department includes all branches of the military and provides a central organizing body for them. The department's Web site offers numerous publications and presentations relating to national security and justification for actions taken by the military.

U.S. Selective Service System
Public and Intergovernmental Affairs
Selective Service System, National Headquarters
Arlington, VA   22209-2425 •fax: (703) 605-4106
e-mail: information@sss.gov
Web site: www.sss.gov

The Selective Service System is an independent federal agency operating with permanent authorization under the Military Selective Service Act. It is not part of the Department of Defense; however, it exists to serve the emergency manpower needs of the military by conscripting untrained manpower or personnel with professional health care skills if directed by Congress and the president in a national crisis. Its statutory missions also include being ready to administer an alternative service program, in lieu of military service, for men classified as conscientious objectors.

Bibliography of Books

James V. Arbuckle — *Military Forces in 21st Century Peace Operations: No Job for a Soldier?* New York: Routledge, 2006.

Beth J. Asch, John Romley, and Mark Totten — *The Quality of Personnel in the Enlisted Ranks.* Santa Monica, CA: RAND Corporation, 2005.

Bruce Berkowitz — *The New Face of War: How War Will Be Fought in the 21st Century.* New York: Free Press, 2003.

John S. Burnett — *Dangerous Waters: Modern Piracy and Terror on the High Seas.* New York: Dutton, 2002.

Lynn E. Davis — *Stretched Thin: Army Forces for Sustained Operations.* Santa Monica, CA: RAND, 2005.

James Dobbins, Seth G. Jones, Keith Crane, and Beth Cole DeGrasse — *The Beginner's Guide to Nation-Building.* Santa Monica, CA: RAND National Security Research Division, 2007.

Michael W. Doyle — *Striking First: Preemption and Prevention in International Conflict.* Ed. Stephen Macedo. Princeton, NJ: Princeton University Press, 2008.

Tod Ensign — *America's Military Today: The Challenge of Militarism.* New York: New Press, 2004.

Matthew J. Flynn — *First Strike: Preemptive War in Modern History*. New York: Routledge, 2008.

Nathaniel Frank — *Unfriendly Fire: How the Gay Ban Undermines the Military and Weakens America*. New York: Thomas Dunne, 2009.

Philip Gold — *The Coming Draft: The Crisis in Our Military and Why Selective Service Is Wrong for America*. New York: Presidio, 2006.

Anthony M. Helm, ed. — *The Law of War in the 21st Century: Weaponry and the Use of Force*. Newport, RI: Naval War College, 2007.

Robert D. Kaplan — *Hog Pilots, Blue Water Grunts: The American Military in the Air, at Sea, and on the Ground*. New York: Random House, 2007.

Deborah C. Kidwell — *Public War, Private Fight?: The United States and Private Military Companies*. Fort Leavenworth, KS: Combat Studies Institute, 2005.

Christopher Kinsey — *Corporate Soldiers and International Security: The Rise of Private Military Companies*. New York: Routledge, 2006.

Jeffrey McGowan — *Major Conflict: One Gay Man's Life in the Don't-Ask-Don't-Tell Military*. New York: Broadway, 2005.

James F. Miskel	*Disaster Response and Homeland Security: What Works, What Doesn't.* Westport, CT: Praeger Security International, 2006.
Charles C. Moskos and John Whiteclay Chambers II, eds.	*The New Conscientious Objection: From Sacred to Secular Resistance.* New York: Oxford University Press, 1993.
Martin N. Murphy	*Contemporary Piracy and Maritime Terrorism: The Threat to International Security.* New York: Routledge for the International Institute for Strategic Studies, 2007.
Robert Perito, ed.	*Guide for Participants in Peace, Stability, and Relief Operations.* Washington, DC: United States Institute of Peace Press, 2007.
Bernard Rostker	*America Goes to War: Managing the Force During Times of Stress and Uncertainty.* Santa Monica, CA: RAND National Defense Research Institute, 2007.
Kathy Roth-Douquet and Frank Schaeffer	*AWOL: The Unexcused Absence of America's Upper Classes from the Military—and How It Hurts Our Country.* New York: Collins, 2006.
Peter Rowe	*The Impact of Human Rights Law on Armed Forces.* New York: Cambridge University Press, 2006.

Harvey M.
Sapolsky, ed.

US Military Innovation Since the Cold War: Creation Without Destruction. New York: Routledge, 2009.

Albert Somit
and Steven A.
Peterson

The Failure of Democratic Nation Building: Ideology Meets Evolution. New York: Palgrave Macmillan, 2005.

James Tracy, ed.

The Military Draft Handbook: A Brief History and Practical Advice for the Curious and Concerned. San Francisco, CA: Manic D Press, 2006.

Rolf Uesseler

Servants of War: Private Military Corporations and the Profit of Conflict. Trans. Jefferson Chase. Brooklyn, NY: Soft Skull, 2008.

Index